Once Upon A Dream

Essex Dream Weavers

Edited By Piers Kitson

First published in Great Britain in 2017 by:

Young Writers Est. 1991

Young Writers
Remus House
Coltsfoot Drive
Peterborough
PE2 9BF
Telephone: 01733 890066
Website: www.youngwriters.co.uk

All Rights Reserved
Book Design by Spencer Hart
© Copyright Contributors 2017
SB ISBN 978-1-78820-422-4
Printed and bound in the UK by BookPrintingUK
Website: www.bookprintinguk.com
YB0327S

FOREWORD

Welcome Readers!

Dreams play a big role in our life, whether from the worlds that keep us entertained at night to the dreams and ambitions we aspire to in the future, so it was only fitting we used this as our topic for our latest nationwide primary school competition.

I am proud to present 'Once Upon A Dream – Essex Dream Weavers', a collection of poetic treasures that will make your imaginations run wild. Among these pages you will find a variety of poetic styles, from dream acrostics to candy land couplets to fear provoking free verse. Some poems may leave you jumping for joy, some may tickle your sides, while others may pull at your heart strings as each author becomes their own dream catcher.

The selection process, while difficult, proved to be a very rewarding task and I hope you enjoy the range of work that has made it to the final stages. With so many wonderful poems featured in this anthology picking a winner was another very difficult task so well done to *Kayleigh Morse*, who has been chosen as the best poet. I'd also like to congratulate all the young writers featured in this collection.

Finally, I hope you find the poems that lie within these pages just as entertaining as I did and I hope it is kept as a keepsake for many years to come.

Piers Kitson

CONTENTS

Winner:

Alysia Last (11) - Myland Primary School, Mile End — 1

Hillhouse CE Primary School, Hillhouse

Zara Ofoma (8) — 3
Murray Anderson (9) — 4
Jesse James Anderson (11) — 6
Sarah Elisabeth ChuFoon (9) — 8
Mary Aldridge (11) — 10
Olivia Fishenden (8) — 11
Evie Wilhemina Majeika (9) — 12
Ellie-Rose Darling (11) — 13
Jairo Templonuevo Castro (8) — 14
Evalina Meek (9) — 15
Skye Keely Morris (11) — 16
Frances Bruton (10) — 17
Amelia Louise Hunger (8) — 18
Keira Dalzell (8) — 19
Lacey-May Knowles (8) — 20
Nathan Collins (10) — 21
Martha Bruton (8) — 22
Albie Pendleton (11) — 23
Tiffany Molly Fairbrass (8) — 24
Tamika Folashade Lolade Bankole (11) — 25
Yaw Yeboah Ohemeng (8) — 26
Naomi Eve Ware (11) — 27
Tracy Abena Owusu-Eyiah (10) — 28
Jssiah Massia (8) — 29
Poppy Louise Anderson (9) — 30
Saawari Taheem (8) — 31
Demi Deaney (8) — 32

Holly Ray (10) — 33
Kimberly Siokwu (10) — 34
Ismet Erbasli (8) — 35
Remi Clark (8) — 36
Oliver Fennelly (8) — 37

Myland Primary School, Mile End

Erin Woods (11) — 38
Ria Hull (10) — 39
Sam Watts (11) — 40
Sheena Franklin (11) — 41
Kimberley Patricia Maclellan (11) — 42
Bruno Brooks (11) — 43
Anne Maria Joseph (11) — 44
Jack Patrick Gostling (10) — 45
Ivan Pearman (10) — 46
W'dron-Oendrik Kundu (11) — 47
Satine Dawes (11) — 48
Sophie Young (11) — 49
Lexi Laura White (11) — 50
Samuel Connor Davies (10) — 51
Harrison Fox (11) — 52
Billy Clarkson (11) — 53
Milly Swan (11) — 54
Shayne Alexander (11) — 55
Frankie Burton (11) — 56
Mianna Catantan (11) — 57
Freddie Boorn (11) — 58
Leo Vicary (11) — 59
Glenn Ryan Naol (11) — 60
Danny Pulham (11) — 61
Alex Stuart (10) — 62

Perryfields Junior School, Chelmsford

Neriyan Tharmathass (9)	63
Daniel McManus (9)	64
Willliam Moore (9)	67
Leon Govus (9)	68
Lily May Nicholls (9)	71
Tia Basi (9)	72
Ruby-Mae Wright (9)	74
Julia Kudlova (8)	76
Freddie Clark (9)	78
Joanie Cheek (9)	80
Ethan Maguire (9)	82
Stanley Spall (9)	84
Andrea Ruchika Hansdak (9)	86
Amelia Westalll (9)	88
James Perrin (9)	90
Anvita Seenivasan (8)	92
Mya Suley (9)	94
Matthew Lawrence (8)	96
Cameron Tingey (9)	98
Holly Garrett (9)	100
Olivia Byrne (9)	102
Krithikha Sriranganathan	104
Dylan Raymond Edward Nowell (9)	106
Nathan Chivas (9)	108
Ethan Moore (9)	110
Aarya Ethan Thomas (9)	112
Emily Barden (8)	114
Izzie Evanson (9)	116
Kitty Lackenby (9)	118
Isabelle Evans (9)	120
Evie Springett (9)	122
Poppy Isabella Farmer (9)	124
Dion Neal Fernandes (8)	126
Grace Louise Bond (9)	127
Charlie Rap Clarke (9)	128
Katie Elizabeth Rudkins (9)	130
Noah Lee (8)	132
Martin Roungkagia (9)	133
Lucie Alston-Baskett (9)	134
Myles Godfrey Hardwick (9)	136
Martin Shaikhly (9)	137
Inayah Asghar (8)	138
Harrison Gooch (9)	139
Liam Johnson (9)	140
Nicole Cornelius (8)	141
David Cardona (9)	142
George Peter Garnett (9)	143
Eliza Cheek (9)	144

St Mary's CE Foundation Primary School, Forest Hall Park

Sophie Springham (9)	145
Georgia June Peel (9)	146
Mia Millest (9)	148
Zak Benjamin Faux (10)	149
Mollie Jaye Thake (9)	150
George Higley (9)	151
Rebecca Trapmore (9)	152
Maggie Cornwell (9)	153
Charlie Connelly (10)	154
William Bafwa (10)	155
Ollie Kiernan (9)	156
Mison Everett-Reid (9)	157
Marie Cornwell (9)	158

St Teresa Catholic Primary School, Dagenham

Archie Macpherson (11)	159
Olivia Grabarczyk (11)	160
Eloise Jenkins (11)	161
Karl Shane Vilar Antipuesto (11)	162
Daisy Makumbi (10)	163

Uphall Primary School, Ilford

Laiba Waqas (9)	164
Zobia Ramzan (11)	166
Mohamed Diine (11)	167
Faduma Ahmed (11)	168
Aye Myant Naing (11)	169
Farhad Muhmmad Arshad (11)	170

White Court Primary School, Great Notley

James Wager (10)	171
Mia Lily Sawyer (10)	172
Sophie Louise Carpenter (10)	174
Samuel Paternoster (10)	175
Jasmine Rockenbach (10)	176
Harry Abbott (10)	177
Layla Huggins (10)	178
Ella Fay Brookes (9)	179
Elodie Dobson (9)	180
Abigail Milner (9)	181
Emily Raven (10)	182
Jack James Adams (10)	183
David Horobin (10)	184
Cameron Dawes (10)	185
Eli Green (10)	186
Callum Orton (10)	187
Henry Payne (10)	188
Tom Parker (10)	189
Harry George Russell (10)	190
Kathryn Edwards (10)	191
Joe Wiltshire (10)	192
Verity Lucas (9)	193
Aishwari Patel (9)	194
Joshua Young (10)	195
Dillon Gold (10)	196
Rhiannon Gray (10)	197
Charlie Haynes (10)	198
Luke Croker (10)	199
Saffron Lily Rose Hockley-Warner (10)	200
Adam Brathwaite (9)	201
Ryan Young (10)	202
Mia Ozcan (10)	203

THE POEMS

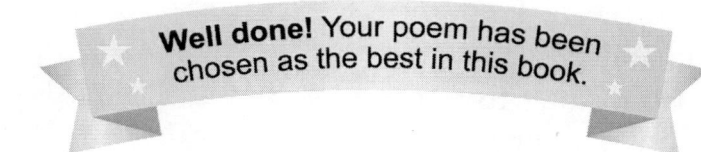

Well done! Your poem has been chosen as the best in this book.

A Whole Other World

I will tell you a dream
A planet that's quite far
To reach beyond the depths
And see the fantasies that are:

Monsters, fairies, goblins
And a giraffe playing a guitar
With candyfloss clouds
Transport in stylish cars

Though one little girl
Decided to venture
To see what it's like
On a real adventure

Jelly Tots as traffic lights
There's slime as the sea
You would start to wonder
What else could there be?

She swam in the slime
Jumped from cloud to cloud
Rode on an elephant
'So fun!' she shouted aloud

Now off she must go
There are galaxies awaiting
Another adventure ahead
Which she's anticipating.

Alysia Last (11)
Myland Primary School, Mile End

Where Am I?

I took an enchanted Pegasus to a nice candy land. I couldn't believe my eyes as it looked astonishing. I asked myself, 'Where am I? Could I be dreaming?'

There were lots of giant chocolate lollies, Candyfloss, Haribos and all the imaginable sweet treats!

I loved the look of the giant candies and wanted to gobble up all of the goodies at once! *This must be a dream island,* I thought. Can life be this fun? If this is a dream, I wouldn't like to wake up.

I got tired of eating candies as I started to feel sick. I wanted to be loved up and there was nowhere in the world to get it other than from my most precious family.

I took my Pegasus back to my beautiful house made out of vanilla cake!

Zara Ofoma (8)
Hillhouse CE Primary School, Hillhouse

And All Went Black

I woke up on a ship
Rocking gently in the wind
Which suddenly turned into a raging storm
And a pirate ship appeared in the distance
It fired at us until we sank
But a captain must go down with his ship
The sea covered my head
And all went black

I woke up in a world of candyfloss and
Unicorns
Rainbows smiling down at us
And all was happy
Then a dragon came
And ripped down trees
All was not happy
Then the dragon came at me
And all went black

I woke up in the war of the Olympians
The goriest place I could have been
In all of history
I seemed to be in the Titan Kronos' body
Wielding a blade of death
I fought ferociously

I sliced
I stabbed
And tried my very hardest
Until a boulder flew towards me
And all went black

I woke up at home
In my nice, cosy bed
I couldn't see pirates, a dragon, or a war
It had all been
Once upon a dream.

Murray Anderson (9)
Hillhouse CE Primary School, Hillhouse

The Dream

As I take an un-thought stroll through the
Corridors with the creaking, sniggering door
I entered the place
With a shivering frown on my face

On comes my blinding flashlight so I can see
Peering around the corner I see
A silhouette with a gun aiming at me

As it goes to shoot
I step back and scream
'It's only a balloon gun,' I say to myself
I carry on walking
It starts to follow me

I start to jog to get away
My jog turns into a run
'Run, run, run,' I say to myself
My run turns into a sprint
I break into a sweat on my forehead
I start to lose energy fast

I begin to slow down
It catches up
I start to get scared
It shakes my hand and it says,
'I only want to be friends.'

Jesse James Anderson (11)
Hillhouse CE Primary School, Hillhouse

Once Upon A Nightmare

Once upon a nightmare
The night is cold and damp
I hide behind a wall
Curl up in a ball

The second I glance behind me
I have to shield my eyes
Alarms are pulsing, screaming
I have to run inside

Charge at the door
Slide across the floor
My classmates are all there
I scramble under a table

I'm next to a friend
I kneel
Is it real?
I dare think it is

Stomping through the door
A tall, dark silhouette
Cigar in his mouth
Wears a trilby hat

He's marching through the room
Lights flicker, flash
He walks out with a child
I hear a crash

Run! my mind screams
Adrenaline pumps through me
Will I ever wake up?
Or am I awake?

Sarah Elisabeth ChuFoon (9)
Hillhouse CE Primary School, Hillhouse

Once Upon A Nightmare

Once upon a nightmare
I'm a tourist, touring Buckingham Palace
Turning a corner
I heard a scream
I'm hoping it's just a dream
But I don't think it is...

Once upon a nightmare
I looked around
The windows shaking
And falling to the ground
I wonder what is going on

Once upon a nightmare
In just one flash
I was gone
Tied up in rope in one corner of a dark room

Once upon a nightmare
Bang!
Dripping with sweat
My arms and legs feel tight
Footsteps coming closer and closer
I hope I survive...

Mary Aldridge (11)
Hillhouse CE Primary School, Hillhouse

Best Dreams

Once upon a dream
There was a unicorn in Candy Land
In Unicorn Candy Land there is a lovely, big candy house
Made out of lovely, bright, clear, melted chocolate, lollipops and bubblegum
The unicorn had lovely bright pink wings that were sparkly
In Candy Land there is also a chocolate fountain dripping into a pool
Unicorns can swim and drink at the same time
It smells like Dairy Milk and cupcakes
The sun always shines no mater what
People are even made out of candy and nothing melts
Beds are made of marshmallows and clouds
And it is a wonderful dream.

Olivia Fishenden (8)
Hillhouse CE Primary School, Hillhouse

My Wonderland

The gleam of a glance in one starry night
The red sun over the horizon as it shone bright
As I got ready to take to the sky
I fear a Chinese dragon as it may fly by
Innocent little creatures unicorns are
Born from the heavens on one wishing star
Every child's dream is to meet a unicorn
As they fear no one
But as far as no one knows they can be friend or foe
Dragons' stone-cold eyes deep with pleasure
When they meet you
But after a while they'll be your treasure
With scales the colour of a rainbow
With razor-sharp teeth as everyone knows.

Evie Wilhemina Majeika (9)
Hillhouse CE Primary School, Hillhouse

The Clowns And The Teacher

Once upon a nightmare
I was alone in class
My teacher, looking at me
Every minute, until one moment
It had been five minutes
No sight of her

I tiptoed out of the room
Then went out the doors onto
The playground
Which was deserted

I looked up and saw
My teacher floating
In the sky
The mysterious figures
In the ocean-like sky had her
Then they descended and I saw
What they were

They were clowns!
I ran inside and locked
All the doors and windows
So they couldn't get in.

Ellie-Rose Darling (11)
Hillhouse CE Primary School, Hillhouse

Magical Unicorn

Above the clouds there are unicorns
Rainbows shining like crystals
Whoosh, went the unicorn, flying above my head
The clouds smile in the sun
Above the clouds there are unicorns
With multicoloured hair
And all have comfortable backs
My unicorn gets lost
Above the clouds there are unicorns
Martha and Abigail are here
They lose their unicorns too
Unicorns can be spotted miles away
Above the clouds there are unicorns
With a mane as silky as ever
Whoosh, went a unicorn under my feet
There are houses made of clouds.

Jairo Templonuevo Castro (8)
Hillhouse CE Primary School, Hillhouse

A Nightmare

Once upon a dream
The skies turn black
A monster creeps by
Covered in smoke

You hear something
Thud, someone moves
Who is it you ask
No one answers

Your voice echoes around
But all you can hear are grumbles
Blackness fills the air
As a monster walks by

Coughing in the darkness
As smoke drifts by
You'll be endangered
So you better wake up

You turn and twist
Dribbling on the pillow
Suddenly you wake up
You are glad it was a dream.

Evalina Meek (9)
Hillhouse CE Primary School, Hillhouse

Once Upon A Nightmare

Once upon a nightmare
In a dark, enclosed room
I stood paralysed in sight of my biggest fears
They were calling for me

Running for my life
I take deep breaths
Waiting to wake up from this horrible mess
They were chasing me

The room's murky corners glowed
As the shadows tiptoed behind me
My fear takes control
The horror of the faces
They're getting closer

My sweat dripping from my forehead
My lungs fill with air
The figure was here
Looking deep into my eyes.

Skye Keely Morris (11)
Hillhouse CE Primary School, Hillhouse

The Astonishing Adventure!

What an adventure I had last night
With weird and wonderful, strange looking sights like:

Candyfloss trains
Rainbow volcanoes
Colourful caves
Murmuring tornadoes
Polk-a-dot tigers
Walking waves
Bungee jumping spiders
Candy canes
Kind teachers
Cowardly lions
Phenomenal creatures
Pink Hawaiians
Flying elephants
Running fish
Leopard skin pants
A wonderful wish

Such peculiar things in my dream
They sound out of this world
But not all is as it seems.

Frances Bruton (10)
Hillhouse CE Primary School, Hillhouse

Fairy Kingdom

Far away in a magical land
A fairy queen lived in a big castle
In the castle there is a glimmering throne
Round the castle are houses shaped like ice creams
Yoghurt cake bridges and stinky cheese hedges
Some fairies are good, some fairies are bad, some have wings, some don't
King fairy was a big fairy in the kingdom
Indigo made everyone laugh
No fairies are sad
Gone! The mean ones are gone. Hooray!
Don't be mean, never be mean
On a hot day fairies come out to play
Morning no fairies are out.

Amelia Louise Hunger (8)
Hillhouse CE Primary School, Hillhouse

Once I Drank A Magical Potion

Once upon a dream
I'm drinking a potion
A magical potion that makes me invisible in slow motion
I'm on a bus, a very fun bus
But I wonder where it's taking me
I haven't asked much
How long is it going to take me?
I'm really in a rush
Is this a candy land?
Let me try one gum
I swallowed a sweet from a house
And it grew back from where I took it from
The houses are made of chocolate cake
Syrup to hold it all together
A lovely chocolate chip biscuit as the door.

Keira Dalzell (8)
Hillhouse CE Primary School, Hillhouse

A Night At Royalty

I had a best dream
Royalty as neat as could be
I met the queen, she is very old
But we made a good start
We slide down rainbows
We went into the royal car
We waved at all the jolly people
We're having fun, it's the best
I met the king, he is very jolly
Is he posh? I don't think so
We went into the royal garden
We did loads of singing
We did some gardening
We had so much fun
I was relieved I found the queen
I was lost, but sadly I woke up, but it was all a dream.

Lacey-May Knowles (8)
Hillhouse CE Primary School, Hillhouse

Nightmare

N ice things don't come from a nightmare
I creep up on a strange figure
G laring at a smoking car
H iding quickly behind a tree
T rembling, I saw him picking up a spanner
M y thoughts changed, now I don't know what he is going to do
A gain, he saw me, he was scared of me, I didn't know if he saw me as a threat
R ealising, I said, 'What's the matter?' He said he needed help to fix the car
E erily, I found myself in bed.

Nathan Collins (10)
Hillhouse CE Primary School, Hillhouse

Magical Flying!

M aking friends along the way
A nd saying city names
G oing along in the sky flying
I n the sky I feel free
C old and whistling breeze blowing across me
A ll I see is clouds
L oads of things I can tell people about my dream

F lying around the world
L ittle amount of people don't like my dream
Y ou are having a dream
I n the world of dreams
N ow you can fly
G lamorous sunlight shines on you.

Martha Bruton (8)
Hillhouse CE Primary School, Hillhouse

The Black Between The Stars

I keep having this dream
That there's something there, the black between the stars
I know it
It can see me... but I can't see it
It sees everything...

It never became, it always has been
It's the enemy left unseen
The shadows reap the courage from my heart
It's taking the light from the dark

It is meaning
It is our life
It makes us one by one insane
With the blade of its knife

I keep having this... nightmare.

Albie Pendleton (11)
Hillhouse CE Primary School, Hillhouse

Dream Land

Once upon a dream there was a land
Where four little girls had a plan
The four little girls were Tiffany, Saawari, Hollie and Emily
Those four little girls are a good team
Emily and Tiffany are as tall as a flamingo
Saawari and Hollie are as small as a dingo
They dreamed they could fly as high as the sky
They dreamed they could glide through the fluffy white clouds
They dreamed big
They dreamed small
But best of all
They had each other.

Tiffany Molly Fairbrass (8)
Hillhouse CE Primary School, Hillhouse

Dreammare

Once upon a dreammare
The world was all dare
You can commit a crime
Without doing any time

Once upon a dreammare
The world full of care
No litter on the ground
No pollution all around

Once upon a dreammare
The world was like a pear
And houses can fly
Like birds in the sky

Once upon a dreammare
The world was all aware
That dogs walk people
And cats are purple.

Tamika Folashade Lolade Bankole (11)
Hillhouse CE Primary School, Hillhouse

Super Dream

S uperhero zooming through the sky, checking to see if there's any trouble
U nidentified, whoo, he is under that amazing mask
P ure and new superhero in Dream City
E legantly flying through the air
R ushing around everywhere

D ashing like a flash
R acing past the clouds
E agle soaring through the air
A iming for the sky
M ost powerful superhero.

Yaw Yeboah Ohemeng (8)
Hillhouse CE Primary School, Hillhouse

Nightmare On The Cruise

Once upon a dream
I was on a cruise going to New York
Suddenly a power cut
What is going on

Once upon a dream
Everybody was gone
Till I saw a tall, slender figure
I tried to look for the lights but no hope

Once upon a dream
Its sinister smile stared back at me
Then the lights turned on
Now everyone is back and Sinister Man is gone

Once upon a dream
I woke up from a nightmare.

Naomi Eve Ware (11)
Hillhouse CE Primary School, Hillhouse

Dreams

A dream is a wish your heart makes
But is that really true?
Does it really wish for a chicken to be eating its own poo?
Does it really wish for your pencil to be coming after you?
So if this is really true please tell me, what do dreams do?

Dreams show the way of love
They show your past and future
And maybe scares
So if you listen closely maybe not prepared
You will know the tunnel of dreams and nightmares.

Tracy Abena Owusu-Eyiah (10)
Hillhouse CE Primary School, Hillhouse

Ninjago: Master Of Spinjers

Once upon a time
I lived on my own
I was training to unlock my true potential
And find out what happen to my family
One morning, as I woke up, a villain was on the loose
So I ordered a costume and it was my favourite colour, green
I tried on my costume and it fit
I went to fight the villain
I tested out my powers and I won
I went back home and straight to bed
I never found out what happened to my family.

Jssiah Massia (8)
Hillhouse CE Primary School, Hillhouse

Fantasy

F or a long time I have dreamt of where the fairies live
A dream that came alive one night and was no longer make believe
N othing so amazing as their pretty little things
T iny houses, trees and flowers and even horses with wings
A sprinkling of fairy dust sends me flying high
S oaring through clouds amongst the birds in the sky
Y ou now know my fantasy dream, of when in bed I lie.

Poppy Louise Anderson (9)
Hillhouse CE Primary School, Hillhouse

Candy Land

In my dream land
People have to have sweets for lunch and dinner
In my dream land
Even unicorns eat candy
The houses are made out of candy like a toffee door, sugar windows
Lollipop flowers, candyfloss bricks
Marshmallow and Smartie stones
100 rooms made out of chocolate, water is chocolate and everything is good
They all grow back and taste even better than before
That is my dream complete.

Saawari Taheem (8)
Hillhouse CE Primary School, Hillhouse

Candy Land

Once upon a dream
In a land of candy
Everyone and everything is made out of candy
Every house is decorated by candy
Trees are made out of lollipops
The banana sweets are the moon
The sun shines every day
People smiling and laughing every day
Beds are made out of marshmallows
Houses are made out of gingerbread
A chocolate pond sparkles in the moonlight

Demi Deaney (8)
Hillhouse CE Primary School, Hillhouse

Once Upon A Nightmare

Once upon a nightmare
I was trapped in a room paralysed with my biggest fear
Its grin as sinister as fear
Its eyes as black as midnight
And its face as white as chalk dust on a blackboard
Then there was blood
Once upon a nightmare
I was trapped in a room paralysed with my biggest fear
The blood dripping from the ceiling like a water leak,
drip, drip, drip.

Holly Ray (10)
Hillhouse CE Primary School, Hillhouse

Miss Fairy

Miss Fairy, Miss Fairy
Where are you?
Katie and I couldn't see you last night
Which gave us a huge fright

Your wings are like a rainbow's mirror
That can be seen from miles away

Let us fly by your side
Ride us into the sunset sky

Miss Fairy, Miss Fairy
Where are you?

Kimberly Siokwu (10)
Hillhouse CE Primary School, Hillhouse

Candy Land

Once a boy went to Candy Land
Everything was made out of sweeties
And candy canes
The boy said, 'How amazing!'
So he ate everything
He had a belly ache
The lamppost was made out of Smarties
It was a dream come true
People were made of Skittles
The boy said, 'Get in my belly.'

Ismet Erbasli (8)
Hillhouse CE Primary School, Hillhouse

Journey For A New House

I got kicked out of my foster home
Because I broke their garden gnome
I... I was adopted, I went and knocked on every door
But no one answered
Until a monster opened the door
Oh, it wasn't a monster
It was a woman
But I still wished I could ignore her
By digging to the Earth's core.

Remi Clark (8)
Hillhouse CE Primary School, Hillhouse

Back To The Dinosaur

I was in the middle of the forest
When I saw I was a raptor
Then I found out I could climb trees
Then I saw a pack of raptors
I jumped then flew past the pack into a tree
I tried to turn but I dropped from the sky on the floor
It didn't hurt and I bounced, I was shocked.

Oliver Fennelly (8)
Hillhouse CE Primary School, Hillhouse

The Worst Night Of My Life!

I'm asleep in bed
Cuddling up to my ted
When all of a sudden I float away
To another day
Where I will never want to be
Because this is my nightmare you see

Clowns walking all over the place
I find myself face-to-face
With something I would never want to see
And never, never want to be

Next I see my parents next to me
Talking about where they think I'll be
Something I would never want to see
And never, never want to be

I'm walking down a dark alleyway all alone
When I see something I wish I had brought my phone
Something I would never want to see
And never, never want to be

I'm back in bed, terrified and scared
I look out my window, I can't stop my stare
I look to see if anything is there
Then I realise it's just a nightmare!

Erin Woods (11)
Myland Primary School, Mile End

Nightmare In The Morning!

Once upon a dream
Or a nightmare I should say
When waking up is only just a sleep away
Horrifying monsters, goblins, owls and clowns
But actually I'm in a deep sleep, safe and sound

Dragons, ghosts and vampires
Hiding behind the doors
I'll never sleep from this day on
From the sound of creaky floors

Shadows in the hallways
Spiders in the bath
The dreams creating very long days
Don't you dare laugh!

Finally, waking up once more
A sudden noise behind my door
Telling myself it's just a dream
Mum said, 'Breakfast's ready, come down Marie!'

Ria Hull (10)
Myland Primary School, Mile End

My Amazing Dream Playing Rugby

As I drift off to the land of dream, I take a glimpse of my bed leaving the ground and transforming into a colossal chocolate bar
Then suddenly my body gets yanked and I'm suddenly in the middle of a rugby match
Now I see I am in the middle of a scrum, fighting for possession over the ball
The ball whooshes behind me and one of my teammates catches it
He swiftly passes it to me as I break out of the scrum and I catch it without messing up
I stretched my legs as far as I can to sprint to the try line to get the Six Nations Cup
I thought how happy my family and team would be
As I dived to reach the try line, my alarm clock woke me.

Sam Watts (11)
Myland Primary School, Mile End

Nightmares

These nightmares wrap their evil hands
Around my soul at night
They start to crawl into my mind
And try to take the light

Twisting, turning in my bed
Then I start to hear a sound
As I try to think of happy thoughts
They still follow me around

Every night I hear a noise
A little girl's screams
I also dream of scary clowns
Who sell candyfloss, it seems

Please just go away
I want happy days.

Sheena Franklin (11)
Myland Primary School, Mile End

Late For School

I'm late for school
Hurry, hurry
Where's my shoe?
Hurry, hurry
Need to brush my teeth too
Hurry, hurry
But wait a second
Breakfast first
Oh no! It's Shreddies
They're the worst!
Run up the stairs
To brush my hair
It looks like a bush
I don't care!
Only two minutes
What can I do?
Ah! There's the other shoe!
I'll get so told off, this world's so mean
My alarm wakes me up, it was just a dream!

Kimberley Patricia Maclellan (11)
Myland Primary School, Mile End

A Child's Nightmare

N othing is more scary than a child's nightmare
I magine all the possibilities
G hastly ghosts chasing you about
H ow do they stop this?
T rembling, they hide in a corner
'M ust be a nightmare,' they tell themselves
A fire-breathing dragon chases them
R unning like the Flash, they run as fast as possible
E xhausted, they faint
S uddenly, they find they're safe in bed!

Bruno Brooks (11)
Myland Primary School, Mile End

Sky High

As I fly
Through the sky
I see a bird
Swooping by
Its eyes are like pools of fire
Its wings are like the sun getting higher and higher.

Next I see
Amongst the trees
The parakeets
Eating treats
Of oranges and mangoes
And pineapples too.

Eventually my trip ends
And so my wings send
Me down to the ground
To sleep safe and sound
And I eventually wake
As my alarm clock shakes.

Anne Maria Joseph (11)
Myland Primary School, Mile End

Football

F ouls being committed, all over the pitch.
O ver to the goalkeeper, the ball lands in his hands, ready to be thrown.
O ver to the defender, he soon seeks the ball, chips it to the striker, who soon takes a shot.
T aking it past the defenders.
B *ang!* In the back of the net.
A ll of the team gathers around.
L ewis gets cheered from all of the fans.
L ewis, your goal was awesome, you deserve it!

Jack Patrick Gostling (10)
Myland Primary School, Mile End

Predator

P etrifying predator in the wilderness
R efrained beasts longing for flesh
E xtraterrestrial beings giving chase ready to kill
D aring as you may be, you can't run
A t times of killing, blood-red, fiery eyes devour your soul
T his time they're here, and not going until they feast
O verpowering, mutilated entities tear you and your dreams apart
R esurrected from the pit itself - Hell.

Ivan Pearman (10)
Myland Primary School, Mile End

Guardian

G uarding you, day and night
U naware they let your dream take flight
A t dusk, they make it full of light
R efined in dreams, nightmare into light
D esire and dreams is their sight
I magine them, just like knights
A nd they'll do anything to make nothing seem white
N ever known, never seen, but they'll always guard your dream.

W'dron-Oendrik Kundu (11)
Myland Primary School, Mile End

What What Dream

A 'what what' dream is a terrible thing
Smiles frown
Sirens sing
And when you're stuck in chocolate cream
All you want to do is scream
But if you're lucky you will see
A 'what what' goat writing a 'what what' note
Suddenly, you open your eyes
And make that dream the one you despise.

Satine Dawes (11)
Myland Primary School, Mile End

My Nightmare...

I started to feel
Like my dream was turning real
I turned around and came across
A broken bridge covered in moss
Suddenly, I heard a noise
It sounded like some haunted toys
Then I heard a creepy laugh
I saw their face, but only half
It revealed itself and then I screamed
Luckily, I'd only dreamed.

Sophie Young (11)
Myland Primary School, Mile End

Dancer!

D ancing and prancing all over the room
A nd leaping in mid-air to and fro
N o one can stop spinning in a loopy loom
C an anyone stop dancing with their heart full of joy?
E verything flicks and flacks, plies and temp lies
R ed, blue, green and yellow flicker and licker.

Lexi Laura White (11)
Myland Primary School, Mile End

Imagine

Imagine a world
Imagine a place
Where nothing makes sense
Not even a race!

Imagine a fellow
With an upside down hat
Well in this dream world
It's normal like that!

And so I conclude
Would you want to live here?
To live in a world
Where nothing is clear?

Samuel Connor Davies (10)
Myland Primary School, Mile End

Vampire

V icious creatures ready to haunt you
A lways thirsty for more blood
M idnight, their powers get stronger
P rey doesn't stand a chance
I ts haunted castle will leave you in a trance
R aising armies to take over the world
E mpire of vampires will rule the world.

Harrison Fox (11)
Myland Primary School, Mile End

Running

Run, run as fast as you can
Under and over is the man
Nowhere to run, nowhere to hide, he will come
Honk, honk, he is here, big, red nose as bright as can be
It's a spooky, scary clown
His grin gets bigger and bigger as I back away
'Boo!' I woke up, it was all a nightmare.

Billy Clarkson (11)
Myland Primary School, Mile End

A Happy Place!

In a calm and peaceful place
With a smile on my face
I dance and skip
Out in the sea
The sun makes it sparkly
The heat beating down
Here, I would never frown
Great things happen here
But then they disappear
It was just a dream!

Milly Swan (11)
Myland Primary School, Mile End

Dreams

D elightful for the people that have them
R elieving stress by the minute
E xtremely fun for everyone
A lways of the best qualities
M esmerising feelings spread up your body
S weet and kind, to the mind.

Shayne Alexander (11)
Myland Primary School, Mile End

Dragon

D angerous creatures of fury and fire
R ampaging high in the sky
A lways hungry, never satisfied
G aining strength every minute
O ver the clouds they fly so high
N ever look a dragon in the eye.

Frankie Burton (11)
Myland Primary School, Mile End

Clowns

C hasing me through the night
L aughing and cackling at me
O n top of me, it smirks grimly
W hen will this torture end?
N ow I am scared, running helplessly
S uddenly I am awoken safe.

Mianna Catantan (11)
Myland Primary School, Mile End

Football

I dreamt I played for Leeds
The final of the cup
I really wanted to score
As it was my debut
The score was 1-0 at half-time
I was afraid we were going to lose
In the last minute
I managed to win it.

Freddie Boorn (11)
Myland Primary School, Mile End

Once Upon A Nightmare

C old-hearted creatures
L ifting me up
O pening my door
W ith his beady eyes he spots me
N ow he leaves me, goes for my best friend
S lowly walking away from me, I ran...

Leo Vicary (11)
Myland Primary School, Mile End

Waking Up

As I lie in my bed
My eyes are closed
Nightmares and dreams
Come and go
Last night to now, I have dozed
My dreams are set, oh so low
I take a sip from my cup
And that is when I wake up.

Glenn Ryan Naol (11)
Myland Primary School, Mile End

Spurs!

S purs are the best
P laying the best football I've seen in years
Yo **U** always see Harry Kane hit one in
R ight in the top bins
S urprising everyone in the stadium.

Danny Pulham (11)
Myland Primary School, Mile End

Sleeping Dino

Dinosaur rests, not a peep
Dinosaur sleeps, relishing his dream
Dinosaur wakes, giving a yawn
Dinosaur sighs, it is now dawn.

Alex Stuart (10)
Myland Primary School, Mile End

The School Of Dreams

As Noah and I majestically swayed around
The beaming sun kindly waved and swayed
A mysterious teleporter appeared and started persuading me like a magician
We slowly stepped out
It was like heaven and hell

The mysterious place in my majestic dream was
Teeming with chocolate, dark chocolate!
With shimmering cream as clouds
And dark, hot lava as sky
A tasty piece of marshmallow crashed down
Onto the golden, laminated floor

We sped like a shiny golden bullet in the sky
While the naughty germs slowly die
It was very, very cold
Noah and I battled a man who is bold
And his name was Boldemoth

We won and earned his friendship
He evilly jabbers like a witch, even though he is a crazy wizard

'Wow!' Oh, it was all just a dream
It's time to have ice cream.

Neriyan Tharmathass (9)
Perryfields Junior School, Chelmsford

Which Dragon

In the clouds there was a wizard
Whose name was Isaac Blizzard
The enchanted location looked fantastic
Like a whole supply of plastic
Toys and video games put together
And it will stay there forever

Suddenly, the fluffy clouds danced from side to side
Then the friend of Isaac's made their houses collide
After that they spoke
They said they would meet at the statue of the old bloke
Then Isaac rushed in his house and stayed as quiet as a mouse

One day Isaac walked with his new friend and talked
Then went to borrow
A brand new wand
Later on his friend left and Isaac met someone
Who did not want to bond
It was a dragon!
He roared with fumes of fire
'Raaa,' he growled next to a wagon

Later he separated into different forms and different colours
Isaac could easily tell some were holograms as some had collars
Faster than cheetahs, faster than birds
Isaac came sprinting saying funny words

'Faoiff tingo, alla fvol ving.'
The first disintegrated, a dragon hologram thing
The others did the same, there were six
There they stood, all a mix
Of colours roaring with furious anger
'Vontea chan,' he yelled
Now there is just one

Ready to fly, the dragon leaped and soared
Out of the marshmallow clouds and flew out of sight
With all his might
Isaac ran and jumped ready to fight
Suddenly, he summoned his beige brilliant broom
And charged in the air like Tom chasing Jerry right through the room

Soon they met and the ruby dragon lost his temper
He started growling, 'Roar, raaa.'
Isaac fought him with no loyal helper
He took him by the neck and they flew

Down from the sky, ever so high
Past the blue birds, past the rocky mountains
They fell
No luck would come from a yell
Time to hire some improvement, so he shot a spell
To make the dragon lose his fire

'Himbo Tee-F,' he shouted
Gasping for breath
The dragon died, it needed fire to live
Now things were looking positive
And the trees started clapping and the wind whistles

He went back to his cheetah
Behind him he opened a heater
And left orange burning things that burst
He had a thirst
Now he had told them the excellent news
There was nothing to lose
He was put in the history books
Next to a futuristic display of hooks.

Daniel McManus (9)
Perryfields Junior School, Chelmsford

Mr Uniballer

I am a unicorn and I want to be a footballer
I may not be able to score goals but I'm good at passing
When I go in goal I headbutt other players, ouch!
Nobody wants me on their team because I don't even wear football boots

So I tie up my boots, put on my shin pads and score goals
The goal doesn't move, only the ball
As the crowd roars, cheering like wild animals

My galloping hooves trotted up and down like jaguars
The other players won't come near me
Because of my large horn

Go, go, go, I tackled like a champion
I go around the players like a dancer
Good old Olly, in goal is sitting there like a boulder
Goal! Mr Uniballer has only gone and scored

Mr Uniballer has made it into the squad
This must be history
A unicorn in a football squad, mental!

Willliam Moore (9)
Perryfields Junior School, Chelmsford

The World Of Everything

For poor little Sam, he'd had a bad day
His enemy had been picking on him and his friend
He was smarmy, a know-it-all and Sam only wished
That he could put the bullying to an end!

All of a sudden, all at once
His bed began to drift
Soon he and his bed flew away
In magnificent haste, so swift

When his bed has stopped running away it disappeared
So he wasn't in his cosy and comfy bed
Sam was in a place with nothing at all
And worse, with Harry, the enemy he dreaded

All around him there was absolutely nothing
Except the annoying enemy
Sam was thirsty so he spoke
'I wish for a giant coke.'

Out of nowhere appeared a giant coke
Much to Sam's delight
Jealous, Harry called out loudly
'I wish for a giant banana I could peel.'

Magically, a giant banana appeared
Making the two burst out in laughter
But remember, the two weren't very close friends
So they were going to be a bit harsher

Sam called out, 'Darty, rarty, party
I wish for a giant army!'
So an army appeared out of nowhere
And headed towards Harry with a menacing stare

Harry screeched, 'Bing, bang, blitz!
I wish for the apocalypse!'
So there was a zombie apocalypse with terrifying heads
Walking towards Sam, they were huge, tall and undead

There were bangs, crashes and booms
Heard throughout the land
Harry was terrified so he screamed,
'Please go and blind Sam!'

All of a sudden, Sam couldn't see
But he could still run, talk and walk
Happily, Sam wished that Harry
Would turn into a giant pork chop!

When Sam had wished that he could see
A magnificent piece of meat stood before him
It was hilarious, seeing that huge, awful boy
Turn into such a ridiculous thing

Soon Sam faded away
After he'd faded, where would he be?
Then shockingly, Sam woke up
It was only just a dream!

Leon Govus (9)
Perryfields Junior School, Chelmsford

Unicorns

The unicorn in my dream is as long as a wooden fence
His colourful horn sprays sparkling paint at me
The unicorn in my dream has a white pearly body
With diamond blue eyes like the ocean

The unicorn in my dream can fly so high like a bird
The unicorn in my dream is well behaved
The unicorn in my dream can stretch its wings so far

He can run very fast and glide
The unicorn in my dream can hear from miles away
The unicorn in my dream ran off to the emerald-green forest
The five unicorns came to help me find him
Bang, something mysterious was going to happen
Then I saw my unicorn
Then this person ran up to my unicorn and killed him
I was very sad, but I replaced him
Then everything faded away

I woke up, it was just an amazing dream.

Lily May Nicholls (9)
Perryfields Junior School, Chelmsford

Beaming The Undefeated Gymnast Forever!

I'm at the Olympics in the O2
My dream is about to come true
All I can see is the vault, bars, beam and floor
My first piece is vault
On vault I'm going first
I'm warming up on vault
It's time to present and do the real thing
I'm in the middle of my vault
I'm jumping on the springboard, wait
Burp!
The springboard burped
My vault was as tight as a knot!
Yes! I got the highest score on vault!
It's time to move on!

Now I'm on bars
I warm up my bars now it's time to present
Bars is my third favourite piece
In my dreams the bar spoke as quietly as a fairy and as quickly as a witch
For my dismount I do a triple straight back with a triple twist!

Now I'm on beam, my favourite piece
In my competitions I just sit back and relax in peace
When I relax I look a bit like a lazy leaf
I was as strong as an elephant
My feet crash on the beam - *crash! Bang!*

It's time for floor, my second favourite piece
Woah! I've never jumped that high in my life
Once I finished my fourth (last) tumble the floor rumbled
I've finished
All we have to do is find out who comes first, second and third!

My friend, Scarlett, came third and my other friend, Grace, came second!
But who's going to come first?
Yes! I've come first!
Hooray!
My dream has finally come true!

Tia Basi (9)
Perryfields Junior School, Chelmsford

The Famous Dancer And Fairy

As I nestled down in my bed
And started to rest my super sleepy head
I began to think of the long day ahead
Then... I was in the icy isle of dreams
'Where am I? Where am I?' I cried in my sleep
I was twirling, leaping, tossing and turning
What? Where am I?
Suddenly, the stage I stood on
Flew up, and just like a diving person
Bang, I fell

Suddenly I was at home in my cosy bed
'Where am I?' I cried
Standing next to me, my fairy friend Sky said,
'Flo, Flo, are you alright?'

A day or two later
I was back up on stage
People shouting my name
'Flo, we love you.'

I leaped off the stage that smiled
Put on my baby-pink tutu
Then twirled back on
The wind whistled through my skirt

Sky leaped on the crimson ribbon stage
'Thank you everyone.'
Then grabbed me and danced off stage

'We're famous, we're famous!' Sky cried
'Oh aren't you amazed
Let's start the next show.'
'OK,' I said

Suddenly
I woke up
I lifted the cover off the shiny, red bed
And saw the baby-pink tutu I had on in my dream
So was it a dream?
I must have slept with it on.

Ruby-Mae Wright (9)
Perryfields Junior School, Chelmsford

The Wonderful World

The unicorn was a magical unicorn
The wonderful world was hot and sunny
Olivia and I were as hot as a light bulb
We were in Animal World
Animals were dancing crazily

The unicorn gave us a tree
In my dream the tree was chocolate and mint
The tree wafted in the beautiful windy, sweating day

The tree in my dreams was magic
Because if we wanted water or food we got it
But something was wrong with it
The plane banged, crashed on the ground

The unicorn gave us powers
We went and saved the world and we saw help
Us two saved a storm with our flying powers
Eliza flew to us but we didn't know
She helped us save the world too

Eliza, Olivia and I went back
We went to the unicorn
We told him everything
The unicorn was proud of us
We were proud too

So we went to the beach
After that hard work
What a celebration!
Bright, bubbly drinks
Chocolate chip ice cream
Amazing time on the beach

Then we went on the unicorn's shiny back
We went in our comfy bed
Then as we woke up
We turned into pretty mermaids
We couldn't walk
So we had a safe ride home

Phew, it was a dream.

Julia Kudlova (8)
Perryfields Junior School, Chelmsford

Candy World!

Suddenly, I fell, until I hit the ground
I got up to see a yellow door
I went up to it and gave it a knock
When the door opened, a man picked up his staff
And turned my cat to stone
My other cat quickly bit his leg
And the man went around the house like a lunatic
I then grabbed his staff and unstuck my cat

My cat let go of his leg
Ran out of the house like a blur
Then I turned around to see a huge half-eaten marshmallow
I realised and turned around
And saw my cat as fat as a boulder

She was so chubby
I had to carry her on my back
We walked down the ginger road
And came across another house
I put my cat down
Went up to the door
And put my cat, Austin, in front of the door
And when the door opened, *crash!*
He was on the floor

But he was thrown off by the man
With holes now in his leg
My other cat, Ally, who was now as fat as a boulder
Started rolling down the hill
She then smashed the house to bits

Then me and my cats were kicked
We flew for miles
And then I woke up from my strange dream
I wasn't happy that I woke up
So I went back to sleep.

Freddie Clark (9)
Perryfields Junior School, Chelmsford

Will Aliens Win?

An alien invasion is what happened the other day
Rescue boats were coming but only a few (maybe two)
Could be saved
Sadly, the aliens were destroying
And there is no one to save you
Except your dog
The strange thing was
Everyone had gone except you and your dog
Where did they go?
You didn't know

The one thing you knew
Was that it was up to you
To save everything
You and your family loves
The beasts were like piles of everything you hate

The wind started singing in the direction of the beast
Bang!
An alien fell to the ground
Where the alien fell there was an earthquake
You discovered their one and only weakness is wind
You wondered how to make wind?

Oddly, the creature started counting to five
Again you were scared, and didn't know what to do
The alien said, '5, 4, 3, 2, 1, gulp!'
The alien ate you!

Ahh! You're in an alien's tummy
Just then you remembered their weakness
You blew gently and...
Boom! Everything inside the creature came out
Mostly because he was sick!
Hooray - yay!

Joanie Cheek (9)
Perryfields Junior School, Chelmsford

The Nightmare

Once I was in a very deep sleep
And then I woke up to hear a bleep
I put my hand on the alarm clock
Then I found my ear was blocked

As I opened the multicoloured curtains
The red, giant sun looked certain
That it was soon going to die
Like everything does in nature

It started to give some burps and crackles
The sun then started to go pitch-black
As it was losing its powerful heat
Then my heart gathered a fast beat

I closed the curtains as quickly as possible
It was such a terrifying sight
Then I ran to my cuddly mum
To tell her what I saw, I must be dumb

This was terribly terrible
This was sadly sad
This was bad, so very bad
Was this the end of our time and the world?

We went to a fully protected bunker underneath the concrete ground
The sun stopped shining and loud sounds occurred
There were sounds of sorrow and death
As the sun went super nova and exploded

This was the end to all life, or was it?
I woke up next morning
Oh, it was just a dream
I felt a lot better after I had a nice cup of tea.

Ethan Maguire (9)
Perryfields Junior School, Chelmsford

Moon Bus

Last night as I was sound asleep
In my ear I heard a peep
It was a tiny voice inside
Although, it wasn't trying hard to hide

The bus was addressed to 67 Moon Lane
It was bright red, like a London bus, just the same
Happily parked outside Perkin's Farm
Loaded with goats straight from the barn!

The pig driver then screamed in surprise
'Today is the day folks, we take to the skies.'
I felt worried, confused and excited
And everyone else seemed hugely delighted!

As we took off and soared into space
I saw that the goats had packed their suitcase
Suddenly, I noticed an evil star
He was racing us and was ahead by far

The star deafeningly cackled a horrible laugh
Then tried stopping us with his gleaming iron staff
Quickly, with great reflexes, Piggy navigated around
Whoosh! We were safe, safe and sound

As we landed safe at 67 Moon Lane
The bright moon smiled, the evil star had caused no pain
Sadly I woke up, the dream had ended
When I next go to sleep it won't be suspended!

Stanley Spall (9)
Perryfields Junior School, Chelmsford

The Extraordinary Thing

Me and my best friends lived on Earth
Both of my friends had the same birth
Then out came an ordinary man
He went and destroyed the land

This thing kept on going on
It started where we came from
And with a strike he got his knife
Then chopped the planet to bits

Then we finally reached Mars
Where the life was weeping at bars
We found a house
Without a doubt
We went walking in

All we wanted to do is discover
But then we took off the biggest cover
Is this house really alive?
Are these pictures tricking my eyes?

This house had some wooden teeth
And emerald feet beneath
There it went, up in the sky
I'm telling you, it isn't a lie!

Crash! Bang! I heard a great clatter
My friends started asking, 'Whatever's the matter?'
I picked up a wand that was on the tough floor
The wands were all sound and the house was no more

I knew this wand was a great believer
So then it struck the planets together
But then I feel over and hit my head
Then I woke up safely in bed.

Andrea Ruchika Hansdak (9)
Perryfields Junior School, Chelmsford

Candy Land And The Royal Unicorn

As I got into my big, blue bed
And slowly laid my head down
As I started my dream
I thought, *what will it be about?*

My gingerbread house that had a laughing chocolate door
And see-through mints
Candy canes and candy food
The yummy bed in my dream

The royal family that live in the gingerbread house
They live with a candy cane unicorn
It was very fast when it was running

'Do not run away
No, no, no, please do not
I am coming.'
Bad, bad

'What is that?'
'It is cool
What is it?'
'Is it what I think it is?'

'Is it a hot tub?'
'No, do not be silly Unicorn.'
'Is it a portal?'
'Maybe, let's go through.'

'What is this place?
Is it an iPhone?'
'No!
I think I have got it
It is a Go Bananas!'

'Let's go back.'
'Yes, that was a bit of fun.'
'No, it was not fun
Because we were only there for ten seconds
And it was just a dream.'

Amelia Westalll (9)
Perryfields Junior School, Chelmsford

Under Your Bed

Scattling and rattling under your bed
Is something red
As you lay down a monster will creep up
And try to nibble a bit off you
He will start to creep up on you and
Roar!

Watch out! Its back is covered with spines as sharp as a claw
If you can smell something weird
Run, it might be a monster
It might have pointy teeth and crinkly knees

Bing! Bang! Wallop! came the banging sound
Of something from beneath the bed

Trickle! Trickle! Trickle! came the swaying noise of the monster
Dripping with hunger and as thirsty as a homeless man
The lights kept on flickering, screaming
As a monster crept out of the bed
And stared up with its fierce eyes

Then he danced his way to the exit
Knocking everything over in his path
Lights, pencil cases and teddy bears

But the most surprising thing
The monster fell down the stairs
And makes a very loud noise
Then when that monster goes home
Another comes out of your toes
Then he starts to stare
So when you wake up you go downstairs.

James Perrin (9)
Perryfields Junior School, Chelmsford

The Magical, Mysterious Chain

Me and my friends were playing at my home
A few minutes later we were playing 'It'
Then, we found a chain that could talk
It took us to a throne (toilet)
It said, 'Flush yourself.'
We actually did flush ourselves
It sounded like *pshsh!*

'Watch out!' said Lily
We landed next to a talking tree
As we looked up, Amelia was screaming
She loved animals
There were unicorns!
Then we found out the chain was magical
The chain changed colours and started to glow!

It took us to a great big palace
We ran inside, there were lots of rooms
All of us peered inside each room
In the last room was the royal family!
I was shocked!
We knocked on the door
Then came running back
'Oh no!'

The alarm went on
The chain was glowing as bright as the sun
This was fun!

We landed in a skateboard park
We were as happy as a lark
We started skateboarding
The chain started to glow
We were home!

Ring, ring, it was all a dream!

Anvita Seenivasan (8)
Perryfields Junior School, Chelmsford

My Dream

Have you ever been to see a wonderful gymnasium?
Well, it's as big as a football stadium
Inside, the noise can make you deaf, it's that loud
Me and my champion are very proud

In the majestic distance the crowd cheered as we walked on stage
The wind whistled through my heart as I hoped to get on the front page
We slowly and carefully got up into prep
On seven I went up into extension
My amazing group took the crowd's attention

The purple and blue uniform when the sun shone
Crystals on the outfit shimmered like the...
Horn on a unicorn
But then suddenly, two flyers fell on the hard floor - *crash!*
One shoe hit someone in the face - *bash!*

The hurt children became furious and wanted to beat the group
So they sprinted away to get some soup
Meanwhile Jack and Jill were losing the will
We were too good
So they put up their hood

The cheer group and I flew back to England
And the cheer group decided to look at octopuses
We lived our lives happily
But did cheer secretly, ssshhh!

Mya Suley (9)
Perryfields Junior School, Chelmsford

Castle

The castle in my dream is like a sword that had just been hardened
The soldiers hide on the battlements
Towers tower as high as skyscrapers
The gates hang on their hinges on the gatehouse covered with ivy

Inside the square keep the royal family
Sat on their gold-plated thrones
Servants run all around the moss covered courtyard
Soldiers practising with their blood-covered, groaning swords
Prisoners rattling bars in the dusty prison cells

The chapel with its magical spire
Always glowed as bright as the sun
Silts on the walls stop arrows from going in
But from the inside you can shoot arrows out

The evil king
Who wants to rule the world
Has chocolate hair and chocolate eyes
Who wants to knock down the castle

Crash, bang, bash
The evil king is destroying
The old eastern wall
The king and queen are worried
Me and my friend hurry to the rescue!

Suddenly everything went black
I was waking up
All around me it was as bright as the sun
It was day.

Matthew Lawrence (8)
Perryfields Junior School, Chelmsford

My Miracle Football Dream!

As I lay on the puffy pillow
My body is bouncing like a marshmallow
I am a footballer playing for Tottenham
It's my dream with my friends

As I'm at Arsenal
The atmosphere is just electrical
As I'm playing for Tottenham
The wind was just like a whistle

1, 2, 3, 4, we're winning again
It's a shame we're not near Big Ben
As I just failed on the emerald-green pitch
My kind grandma went and got me some biscuits

As I go and save four goals
My mum handed me a mini roll
Even though I feel really nervous
All my family are here to support me

As the loud whistle goes
The tunnel flows
Everyone wants my autograph
It just makes me laugh

As we're on the bus going home
I heard my mum on a microphone
As we arrived back at White Hart Lane
I saw my Lamborghini near a drain

As that twelve hours passed
It's my turn to say bye-bye
As I wake up in my dressing gown
I just realised, it's all a dream.

Cameron Tingey (9)
Perryfields Junior School, Chelmsford

Bad Unicorn Dream

As I lay on my pillow
There was a unicorn
With a rather large horn
There was a bumblebee

It walked towards me
A mystical, magical unicorn is what I want to be
What a shock, it took my smoothie
I was only gong to watch a movie

Why was there a unicorn?
It was only dawn
Boom! It was staring right at me
Its horn was full of poison
It hurts just like a sting from a bumblebee

Down to the floor I went
My legs were bent
What to do
I was covered in goo

Out came a rainbow from her horn
What a strange unicorn
I want to go home
I am all alone

I was hiding behind a palm tree
Where is the bumblebee
The unicorn is full of danger
Who is this stranger?

I want to go home
I am all alone
I am still behind the palm tree
There is the bumblebee

What shall I do?
There is nothing to do
I woke up because of a light beam
What a strange dream!

Holly Garrett (9)
Perryfields Junior School, Chelmsford

Miss Rainbow Sparkles Dancer

As I frantically danced
I had a magical chance
That magical chance was to imagine what I wanted to be in my dream
I thought and I wanted to be in the dreamy unicorn team

And so I went sleepily to my bed
I woke up with a multicoloured unicorn horn on my head
Everybody questioned and questioned
But I never ever mentioned

Rainbow Sparkles is my majestic unicorn name
Very soon people might get to know me and I might get the fame
I still pranced and danced in my happy place
But people never recognised my face
As I was laughed at I walked out of the room
But they followed and they started to shout, 'Boom Boom.' (Which means boo in unicorn language)

A tear fell from my face
And I ran out with a pace
As my eyes opened I was a little shocked
I opened the door

And a little sadness came over me
That's when my mum shouted from downstairs,
'Are you OK, you were talking in your sleep.'

Olivia Byrne (9)
Perryfields Junior School, Chelmsford

Magic Land

Magic Land is a wonderful place
Like shivering jelly in a case
Everything there is treasure
No one is under pressure
It's absolutely divine
Now one day, it was Queen Alacorn's birthday

It's either April or May
All the animals were gathering
To see what was wanted of them
Scream! Shout! Everyone had ideas

'Stop!' shouted the chief, who was annoyed
They were all in silence until a train ran by
They were going to make a surprise
To see the sparkle in her eyes

She would love it, they were sure of that
Although they acted normal
The looks on their faces nearly gave it away
The queen was suspicious

Under the misty moon
It was as cold as ice cubes
But just as Queen Alacorn stepped in the water meadow

Surprise!

The queen was so happy
She lit the night with her horn
Fireworks burst and filled the night-black sky with bright fireworks.

Krithikha Sriranganathan
Perryfields Junior School, Chelmsford

Circus

Once in my dream lived a boy reading a poster with his dog
While sitting on the couch
The comic said, 'Go to the circus, no need to pay'
And before you knew it, he was gone, he didn't bother to stay
He was already in a seat
His heart was going beat, beat, beat
He was the only one there
When all of a sudden, a massive bear
Sprouted four legs
The tent even gasped
At the sight of an eight-legged bear
He wanted to speak but he didn't dare
Luckily, it disappeared in a flash of light
Then a clown came in with a fright
He said, 'Where is my nose?'
Then he struck a pose
Timmy's nose pulled a face and shot off his nose
And bounced off his nose to the clown's posing nose
Timmy ran out of the circus crying
His dog was flying
All the way home, where they finished
Sitting on the couch

Beep! Beep!
Yawn! It was just a dream, phew
I hated that!

Dylan Raymond Edward Nowell (9)
Perryfields Junior School, Chelmsford

Strange World

I find myself in a portal land
With a big, fat band
The sky is green
And the trees hung

Just wanting people to walk into them
And birds flying at my feet
Red pigeons and blue parrots
As colourful as can be

Houses on clouds
Grow and scrape
But clouds disappear
And houses make new ones

Yetis and dinosaurs
Roam the sky
And I
Was a god

If I wanted a pet yeti
I would have one
I was so powerful
I could have
A pencil and rubber
Which could rub things out

And draw stuff
Like the king's riches
And an army of zombies
Or angry idiots

But one day
A boy called Harry
Found the pencil
And he drew a zombie army and another Harry
So I came along with a rubber and
Rubbed out both Harrys
And the apocalypse
And rubbed out his
Footprints and his house.

Nathan Chivas (9)
Perryfields Junior School, Chelmsford

A Nightmare

When I went to bed my brain popped out my head
I entered a dream
But I was at the end of the world
Boiling soup was pouring down from groaning clouds!

Eventually, the rain stopped in mid-air
I could just about make out a figure
I got out my sword and shield
I was ready for evil magic all along!

Instead the figure was in the distance
The figure grew as it came closer
The figure was a zombie
The zombie was exotic but evil!

The zombie was wearing a tattered red robe
The zombie was pink like candyfloss
With menacing eyes
Of course the zombie was bald!

In a fright
I turned on the light
And killed the zombie outright
But I was scared the whole night!

My mum went, 'Boo!'
And I went, 'Ah!'
I told her about my dream
So she had a nightmare and she turned into cream!

Ethan Moore (9)
Perryfields Junior School, Chelmsford

The Cricket Dream

The green grass is moist, ready for play
I feel the ball, new for the day
Running like Usain Bolt wearing the sea
I bowl my first delivery!

The multicoloured marshmallows tremble in fear
When, *crash!* They fell over!
Walking back with the sun smiling at me
Hoping my family celebrate with glee!

In the crowd, a multicoloured wave spread
Like mixed fruit jam on bread
The tranquil pitch was wet
Like a river caught in a net

Out came Abhi Lucking
Good at batting, good at whacking
When I bowl my next ball
I stumble then I fall

Lucky for me
It's a good delivery
Straight, hitting the middle stump
The leather ball collides with a bump

The next ball is good for cricket
I would be lucky for a wicket
Straight for a catch in the deep
When I suddenly wake from my sleep!

Aarya Ethan Thomas (9)
Perryfields Junior School, Chelmsford

My Olympic Dream

What would it be like in the Olympics?
I think it will be so terrific
I will love to start on the bars
I will love to fly all the way to the stars

Next I will make my way to the beam
To win this would be a dream!
If I fall
I will not fail
I will just take a deep breath and exhale

The third event that I will succeed in is the vault!
The vaulting table roared in fear as I bolt
I jump off the springboard like it is a catapult
I fly through the air like a butterfly
Over I go
1, 2, 3, land it easy as can be!

Now I shall begin my first tumble on the floor
As I finish my first tumbling pass
I was quite bored
As the floor rumbled with joy
I hope that I am better than a boy

Over all we can say
I came first
Gracie came second
Isla came third
My dream has come true.

Emily Barden (8)
Perryfields Junior School, Chelmsford

The Monstrous Moon

The monstrous moon
You make us feel gloom
For as we loom onto you moon
You lose the gloom of your monstrous moves
The grooves in your shoes
Come out of the gloom
As your monsters move to get you
You jump on the train
As fast as you came

You fetch your cane
Driving fast away
Towards the day
All dressed in grey

Ghosts call your name
Whilst the others cackle away
And you drive far away
From your monstrous cave

The monstrous moon
Now *you* feel gloom
For we loom towards your moon
To destroy all you have used

All you have done
Has made us glum
For now you feel our slum
We shall invade your fun

I hear an alarm
Waking up the charm
Of my adventure on the moon
And the gloom in it too, I wake up with an achoo!

Izzie Evanson (9)
Perryfields Junior School, Chelmsford

A Ballerina Creation

I was asleep on my pillow
My dream had awoken
I woke up in a place different and unspoken
I was there with my friends, Holly and Lucie
In a mansion so pretty
It was spotlessly clean
So clean that it smiled at me!
No footprints had been painted on the walls or beneath
The floor, lovely marble and a golden staircase
Oh goodie!
I walked up the stairs
It had no particular height
And there was a mirror at the top of the flight
I saw my reflection
But oh, it wasn't me
It was a beautiful ballerina
And a tutu to make her complete
Was it really me
Yes, yes it was
I was a ballerina
My wish had come true
I danced and I danced till I was too tired to speak
I did one million shows in a day or two

Now I'm awake
The picture has gone
I was actually myself all along!

Kitty Lackenby (9)
Perryfields Junior School, Chelmsford

A Dream

In a world with no fear
Happiness will always be near
The sun will shine
And every sentence will rhyme

Deep in a forest
Of multicoloured trees
There is a zoo and a lock
You will have to open with keys

A purple cow will go *moo!*
A flying pig will go *oink!*
An owl will go *twit-twoo*
And a sick giraffe will go *zoink!*

And as night falls
The animals will become tiny
Above their heads are stars
That are bright gold and shiny

Their pupils will grow miniscule
And they will turn crazy and wild
They are as dangerous as a lion
And their friendliness is mild

The frightening hog will grunt!
The pitch-black wolf will howl!
The fearsome tiger will *roar!*
And the golden lion will *miaow!*

Isabelle Evans (9)
Perryfields Junior School, Chelmsford

Unicorns

An upside-down world with unicorns to pet
An enormous world with glitter and candy to enjoy eating
The tie-dye unicorns have magical powers so they don't need a vet
And some special candy even has feet!

There are rainbows like shimmering stars
And clouds like soft cotton
There is a castle made of chocolate cupcakes
A cupcake castle you could say

But a witch came along and accused you
You know what you did
You ate too may sweets
Oh no!

The wicked witch put you in a cell
Now I will make sure you don't go hungry
Have some sweets!
You soon realise she has made a very bad mistake
She gives you strawberry laces
You tie the laces together

And lasso the gold-horned, dancing unicorn
It sets you free
Yippee!

Evie Springett (9)
Perryfields Junior School, Chelmsford

The Royal Golden Toilet

Why do toilets look so evil?
Why do toilets have weevils?
Why do toilets have golden rings?
Why do toilets sometimes have wings?

The bossy king woke one morning
And went to his toilet and was disappointed
He said, 'It's golden,'
And sat on it
But the toilet was not happy
And flushed him down!

He woke in a brown house
He was the King of
The Poop Land
And never lost his throne

The servants had brown hair
And smelt a little whiffy
They had pearl white skin
That melted every second

But the king had to go
And meet his family
As they arrived in Poop Land
And none of them ever came back

Now I just woke up
That's the end of my dream
It was a lot of fun
What a strange dream?

Poppy Isabella Farmer (9)
Perryfields Junior School, Chelmsford

Zoo Adventure

The zoo in my dream is as big as Brazil
The animals in there can never keep still
One night, I mistakenly sleepwalked and ended up in a zoo
And got locked up in there for a day or two!

When I woke up, I found myself on a pile of hay
I bent over the side of my bed and looked for my breakfast tray
Where was it?
Argh, I wasn't on my bed
I lay outside a shed!

The poor animals slept in their bars
Like calm magic locked up in jars
I found a key lying next to me
So I set free a chimpanzee

In a minute all the cages were open
Now that was done
The gates were going to unlock
This is the hilarious moment

Soon the gates unbolted and all the animals ran free!
So the visitors had nothing to see
Except for me!

Dion Neal Fernandes (8)
Perryfields Junior School, Chelmsford

The Land Of Glitter!

Once upon a time, there was a land named Glitter Land
It was named Glitter Land because it was so grand
There was always a rainbow, that's why it was obviously so beautiful
My friends looked at my amazing waterfall

The wonderful candy tree drops delicious ice cream
Also my pink and purple candy castle gleams
Warm, fluffy marshmallows slowly float down from the multicoloured sky
All of my cute, little rainbow minions ask me why

Every day I wake up with pink, purple, blue and silver glitter everywhere in my chocolate fountain
All of my minions complain because they have to climb a mountain
Me and my best friend go in the pool
Which is full of glitter
My nan comes round and by the way, she's a professional knitter.

Grace Louise Bond (9)
Perryfields Junior School, Chelmsford

A Magical Toad

One day there lived a toad
That was close to a long road
Then he saw something he'd never seen
'I haven't seen this, where has this been?'
Then a lake went bang
So a little frog quickly ran
Then the toad slipped in
Often like a banana skin

The toad landed in outer space
With a very, very nervous face
Then he met the sun
Who had a burger bun
The sun said, 'Hello.'
But then came a buffalo (typical)
The buffalo said, 'Bye-bye,'
As he sighed
But then came a little frog
Who hid behind a log
'I am the frog who ran
When the lake went bang
My name is Bob
And I have an important job.'

He fell
'Nooooo!'
It's all a dream. Wow!

Charlie Rap Clarke (9)
Perryfields Junior School, Chelmsford

The Day I Became A Famous Gymnast

Imagine what it would be like to become a famous gymnast.
Imagine what you could win!
This would be the best moment of your life!

I always start on vault,
I jump right up high,
It makes you feel like you have just been pinged out of a catapult,
I twisted and turned over the top,
As I landed on the floor and rumbled with joy.
Boom, bang, pop!
Why do humans jump so high?
Why do people never fly?

Next I start on bars,
I twist and turn right over the top.
I point my toes,
Then I land softly.

Next I'm going to beam.
I jump on top.
And launch my round off back tuck.

Next I went to floor.
I ran and ran as fast as a cheetah.
And that was the day I became a gymnast!

Katie Elizabeth Rudkins (9)
Perryfields Junior School, Chelmsford

The Flying Lamborghini

The Lamborghini flew though New York like a speeding bullet
But suddenly, spiders fell from the sky
But they fell and they died!
As we flew through the sky
We ate some apple pie!

As we parked at the stadium
We went on the playing field
The Lamborghini was very cold
So we flew to someone old
But Charlie was with him
Then the lights became very dim
After the lights went very dim
Charlie accidentally broke his limb

Lamborghini found a finger spinner
Then he wanted some dinner
But he remembered that Charlie broke his limb
So he drove back to the stadium
Crash! Stomp! Crash!

As I realised it was all a dream.

Noah Lee (8)
Perryfields Junior School, Chelmsford

The Futuristic Space City

Finally, I reached the enormous city in space
But the problem here is that I don't have an emerald mace
The tradition in this city is very simple
When there is a new person in the city
They fight the mighty hyena alien
And if they defeat it they become king or queen
There is a very special emerald in the middle of the city
But only if you defeat the mega dinosaur alien robot
You may gain its powers and you might gain a clue

The wonderful space city was bright blue and red
There might even be bright pink at the end
Crash! Bang! The black clouds roared
The dinosaur came out of the woods
And got a basketball and scored.

Martin Roungkagia (9)
Perryfields Junior School, Chelmsford

The Competition

In my dream
I can stretch and lean
I can dance and flip
With a swollen lip
I run to my studio
To put on a show
The stage is ready to dance and flip with me!

I rush onto the stage
To make the crowd amazed
I cartwheel and spin
When I begin
Now it's time for the tricky part
Very far from the start
I did it perfectly!

The show is coming to an end
With the very last bend
And the last twirl
And the very last swirl
It is time for them to choose the winner
The one that was the very best spinner
And guess what, I won!

Then I opened my eyes
And I realised
It was all just a dream!

Lucie Alston-Baskett (9)
Perryfields Junior School, Chelmsford

Horror!

The house in my dream is as tall as a mountain
And the bricks are as hard as a stone on a fountain
The house is my dream is like a ticket to Hell
The house in my dream is horror with a little bell

Crash, bang, wallop, a tiny piece of engineering falls to the ground
We get up and send out the snarling hound
Ralph sniffs out the monster and runs back to us
Ralph barks outside the house
We get up and jump on the bus

The beast was as brown as a big bar of choco
We couldn't do anything, with just a small rock
Beep, beep, beep, beep, beep, click
'Oh phew! It was just a dream.'
Or was it?

Myles Godfrey Hardwick (9)
Perryfields Junior School, Chelmsford

Candy Land

As I was in a deep, deep sleep
Somebody whispered in my ear, 'Psst.'
I backed up startled against the wall
In shock I fell through, it was a zip slide

I landed in a carrot cake house
I stepped out of my scrumptious house
I went to go and meet Mr and Miss Gingerbread Man

'Why are you in my mint-green garden?'
He shouted,
'And what are you doing?'
'I don't know.'

They had ruby-red walls
And snow-white ones as well
There was mud that tasted like honey
There were strong liquorice fences
Whoo whoo, what just happened
It was a dream.

Martin Shaikhly (9)
Perryfields Junior School, Chelmsford

A Strange Candyland

I was sitting down on a chair
In my yard
As a strange portal appeared
Out of nowhere
I stepped through the portal
It led me to Candyland!
Which was very grand!
When I was in
I saw some people walking around
They were spending their pounds
The bright golden sun shimmered
As I came across a house
I knocked on the door
Of a gingerbread house
I waited for a long time
Until a strange-looking lady appeared
I went inside
She looked a little weird
She offered me a nice cup of tea
It looked amazing so I said, 'Yes please!'
I drank the tea and I thought, *it's time to ski.*

Inayah Asghar (8)
Perryfields Junior School, Chelmsford

The Train Of Hell

The blood-red train chugged along the track
As I found a jet-black spider on my back
Crash! The train smashed into a tree
The wheels were as small as a pea

The freaky tree waved at me
Because I needed a key
The clown wanted to play with my ball
The train was as long as a high school

Ghosts were everywhere, haunting me
As I reach for the shiny key
Explosions came from outside the train
I had a big cane

Suddenly, I saw a huge claw
As I stepped through the chocolate door
I swiftly jumped out of the way
Slowly I woke up to see the light of day.

Harrison Gooch (9)
Perryfields Junior School, Chelmsford

The Dream Tree

The tree in my dream is as tall as a skyscraper
With branches, thick like a sports car
The tree in my dream has a golden staircase and a slippery slide
With emerald leaves and a donkey for rides

Pop, moan, squeak, here come the gummies
Washing down ice cream, diamonds and money
Through the gaps in the tree the sun bounces through
Shines upon Mr Sprinkles and his crew

A few minutes later, a magic tomato with wings flew past the tree majestically
I followed it and it led to Tomato Land
When I got there I saw a snake but the music sounded like animals in a cage.

Liam Johnson (9)
Perryfields Junior School, Chelmsford

Dreams

Famous fairies
Dinosaurs with horns
Chocolate fountains
On top of mountains
Dreams are anything you want them to be

Spider athletes that run in a race
Slow slugs keeping up the pace
Dreams are anything you want them to be

Flying footballs
Monster writers
Crash!
Thud!
Crash!
Thud!
The monster of Dream Land comes out
And yells, 'Don't hide
Dreams are anything you want them to be

My mum came to the rescue by waking me up
And saying, 'Wake up sleepy head!'
Phew! That was close.

Nicole Cornelius (8)
Perryfields Junior School, Chelmsford

The Wave

As the night goes by
Time will fly
Monstrous creatures will rise
What a surprise

Werewolves howl but they're not your pal
At the end of the corridor I see a razor-sharp claw and a hairy paw
I ran and ran and never looked back
I ran and ran, then saw a brown shack

As I opened the door
I saw a claw that was on a hairy paw
I screamed like a woman and ran though the door
I ran for my life
And grabbed a sharp knife
I ran and ran as fast as a fan
I saw a sharp fang
And heard a loud bang
The werewolf was steady
But I wasn't ready.

David Cardona (9)
Perryfields Junior School, Chelmsford

Raining Stones

Quick, get inside as the stones smash
Our car has crashed
And the windows are smashed
Smash! He hit me with a bash

Whack! We broke a chair and put it over our heads
To protect us from the big stone called 'Neds'
We had to quickly get to our beds
The next day we saw more Neds

The safe house was a mile away
There was a sculpture made from clay
We went the right way
It was a very long day
Suddenly, a wizard opened the door
He hit me and said, 'Roar!'
Wow! It was just a dream.

George Peter Garnett (9)
Perryfields Junior School, Chelmsford

The Fairies Question

The fairies were dancing, one of the fairies said
'What are you doing?'
They were not nice fairies
She giggled an evil laugh
'Don't go away, come back.
Come back!'

'Your brown, dark hair can never be seen
Just like a little bit of brown dark tea.'
She giggled her evil laugh as happy as can be
Now she is gone, never to be seen
Can't I see she is scared of me?
Oh no, stuck on an island, frothy pink ice cream for tea

I wake up, just a dream
I was scared as can be

Eliza Cheek (9)
Perryfields Junior School, Chelmsford

Fairy Footballers

The fairy footballers are getting bullied
On the green-grassed pitch
The four-leafed clovers are not an inch high
But a millimetre tall
Right for their height

I am sitting in the box
With the referee overhearing the conversations
The fairy dancers are bullying the footballers
One of them said, 'Let's have a game.'
One footballer said, 'Alright, tonight.'

That night, the game was on
I felt scared, excited, curious
And eager to find out who wins
The fairy footballers came out on the pitch
The crowd went wild but the fairy dancers came out late, 'Boo!' they cry

They blow the snail, the game started
Now it is one-all
The fairy footballers score a goal
The fairy footballers win
'Score!' they shout
The game is lost and won!

Sophie Springham (9)
St Mary's CE Foundation Primary School, Forest Hall Park

The Unicorn Ride

Come here, little unicorn
I see your bright light
What a wonderful surprise
Seeing you this time of night

Please let me ride you
I'm not like a kangaroo
I won't bounce, nor hurt
There is only one thing though
I don't like dirt!

So let's get ready
Ready for a ride
Go, go, go unicorn
I'm ready for a dive

Whoohoo! This is so much fun
But where are we now?
There are lots of unicorns
Oh no, please don't say we're going down!

I want to go back home now
Little unicorn turned around
She flew me all the way back
To my amazing, colourful town

I ran to my purple front door
And then said, 'Thank you for the ride.'

I started running to my bed
But then my baby sister cried
I got spotted by my mum
I woke up in a fright
It couldn't be just a dream
Could it?

Georgia June Peel (9)
St Mary's CE Foundation Primary School, Forest Hall Park

The Missing Unicorn

I am a unicorn shining bright at night
We seek to find our friend with all our might
I hope she comes back soon or I will get a fright
She will come back even if it's not light

My heart is in the right place
Even though I don't know how to tie a lace
You always used to beat me in our race
I still remember your shimmering face

I can see the dream land over there
Where people come to look, but then stare
Can you see the sunflowers' glare?
But, 'Ahhhh!' They're running around the fair

That can't be her, could it?
Shining in that bright blue kit
The one that she let me knit
It couldn't be her, could it?

Mia Millest (9)
St Mary's CE Foundation Primary School, Forest Hall Park

A Nightmare Like No Other

N othing has appeared, it's strange, I can't see
I step forward, I see a light, oh no, it can't be!
G o look at the beast, it looks back, steps in the smoke
H ow? Who? Why is it here? It must be a joke
T ap! Something is behind me, I have to look around
M y fears have found my dreams, it's a frightening clown!
A hh! I nearly had a heart attack, I saw its grim face
R unning as fast as Flash, I heard a bang, it was the chase
E yes are glowing out of nowhere, I can't believe I'm not dead
S uddenly, my eyes open, I'm in my bed, still it was nothing but dread!

Zak Benjamin Faux (10)
St Mary's CE Foundation Primary School, Forest Hall Park

My Favourite Dreams

There are a lot of dreams in mind
But sometimes I have to chose mine
I have topsy-turvy dreams
Flying all around
Meeting new friends
And having a new crown

Dreams can take you anywhere
You can go to Neverland
People can shrink in small holes
Or even meet Peter Pan!
Go on stage
Dance about
Then go upside-down

But sometimes you have
Nightmares
Like finding poisoned spiders
Or eating rats and having a fire
Or being rolled like a tyre!

Dreams are not all bad
Never think they are
Never hate a dream
You might have a laugh.

Mollie Jaye Thake (9)
St Mary's CE Foundation Primary School, Forest Hall Park

Mythical Beasts

M onsters, dinosaurs, the lot
Y ellow dragons, I feel like I'm in my cot
T he wizards, the unicorns, the pirates
H ilarious, goofy clowns
I want my pet grey hound!
C laire, help me!
A thlete, that's what I am
L oyal to my country

B oston, that's where I'm from
E erie, twinkling streets, filled with mythical beasts
A ll the creatures gather here, demi gods, yetis
S uddenly, I fall down a drain
T he surprise I got when I landed
S cylla, that's what I see!

George Higley (9)
St Mary's CE Foundation Primary School, Forest Hall Park

My Night Terror

N ight is upon us now
I take a breath to calm myself, but the moon
G rins at me like a clown
H owling like an alarm clock, the wolf came for me
T earing all my clothes, I'm running in the holes

T he shadows coming fast
E very time I look at him I see his sickening grin
R unning as fast as I can, I reach the end of the hole
R ound me just a dead end of darkness, oh no! I'm in the wolf's den
O ver me was a wide-mouthed wolf, ready to gulp!
R ight away I woke, warm in my bed.

Rebecca Trapmore (9)
St Mary's CE Foundation Primary School, Forest Hall Park

My Dream I Never Had

My dream I never had
A dream that I never thought I will never have
My dream will come true tonight

I am here, I'm actually here
I see dazzling ballerinas everywhere
But the weird thing is, every time they jump, they fly up in the air

I signed up for lessons
But I have to do a lace, but I have to go on with no lace
I got in
I'm happy, I got in
First we got on the floor
I want to get better
I did it
I am here performing on stage
I'm here performing Swan Lake.

Maggie Cornwell (9)
St Mary's CE Foundation Primary School, Forest Hall Park

Travelling

Once upon a dream
I find myself getting out of a car
And I look up, what do I see but
London Stansted airport
I get giddy with excitement
But right in the back of my mind
I think, *why am I here?*
But then I hear a voice,
I know who it belongs to
It is my best friend, Eoin
We get through security
But the next thing I know
I am on a plane not knowing
Where we are going
But suddenly without warning
I wake up
I think to myself, *what?*
That was a great dream!

Charlie Connelly (10)
St Mary's CE Foundation Primary School, Forest Hall Park

My Nightmare, The One I Hated

N othing I know about
I can't stop running, it's as if someone is haunting me
G lowing in the horizon, I see shadows which appear to be monsters
H owling at me, what does this mean?
T rying to grab me, I'm attempting escape but they won't let me
M y mind is thinking my life is over
A m I cursed for doing something wrong?
R isen my heart was, when will this stop?
E ventually, all the noise stopped, it was just a nightmare, the one I hated.

William Bafwa (10)
St Mary's CE Foundation Primary School, Forest Hall Park

Shrunk Down

S hrunk I am, but I am riding my dogs
H igh up on
R oxy, Ruby, Freddie, I can see fleas in a UFO
U ntil I shoot it with a bow
N ow everything's turned black
K *aboom!* The smoke came from the UFO, it flew

D own into my kitchen and I'm still riding my dogs
O n an adventure to kill the fleas
W ow! It was a dream
N ow I know it was, I am sad.

Ollie Kiernan (9)
St Mary's CE Foundation Primary School, Forest Hall Park

Dragons

D ragons stare deep into eyes of brave Vikings
R unning for their lives, the scared Vikings run from the dragons
A menacing dragon I see in front of me
'G o, save yourself,' I tell my brother, 'I'm not important'
O n the floor I smell a smell of fish guts, urgh!
N oises shrieking behind clouds
S cales dropping on my head like dandruff.

Mison Everett-Reid (9)
St Mary's CE Foundation Primary School, Forest Hall Park

A Dancer Dream

I am a dancer and I love to dance on stage
Sometimes I think I can do anything
I've got a lead but my shoes have gone
Where did I go?
I'm in a land with unicorns and pongs
And rainbow and fairies
And I'm in a lovely dress

I meet a fairy, her name was Toffee Cake
She had some shoes for me to take
I ran to the unicorns and I go and find out
It was all a dream.

Marie Cornwell (9)
St Mary's CE Foundation Primary School, Forest Hall Park

I Am A Superhero

I had a dream that I was the most awesome Flash

A nd I was saving thousands of cities in a dash

M etahumans getting defeated, definitely doesn't earn me any cash

A m I going to be able to be the victor? I need to win

S isco Ramone makes cool and weird weapons like the... bin

U hh... he also made the thing that transforms people into a tin

P eople who I work with are called the Justice League, they're cool

E veryone thanks us for our heroics, we have our own pool

R onnie is Firestorm, he blasts fire and he is cool

H eroics is my middle name, I like to toss lightning

E ventually, I'll be running at mach 8 and I'll be winning

R onnie suffered a fate worse than death and now Katelin's crying

O ver is what it is now, oh wait, now there's a paradox called Flashpoint.

Archie Macpherson (11)
St Teresa Catholic Primary School, Dagenham

Black Hole Danger

I had a friend wizard and he said he liked me
His name was Wizard Bee and he was 103
Once he told me to get some mushrooms from the forest
I don't believe he was actually honest
So I went there and collected them
All of a sudden I heard a big trem
It raised me up and dropped me down to the ground
My head was going round and round
Suddenly the forest got dark and I accidentally stepped on a strange mark
Soon I got lost but I still walked forward
Then I yawned and got slightly bored
There was a black hole in front of me and I didn't see it
So I walked on it carelessly but didn't mean it
Suddenly, I started falling, falling, falling...
I closed my eyes but my heart kept stalling
Then I woke up and found myself in my bed at home
My family came to me and talked about Rome.

Olivia Grabarczyk (11)
St Teresa Catholic Primary School, Dagenham

The Mad World Of Unicorns

This wild creative world is such a wonder
But I wish there could not be the deafening thunder
I look around and see a world of great madness
Unicorns are everywhere all shapes and sizes

They all have something special
My one has to be shiny and purple
I spot a gigantic purple building in the distance
I head towards it and on my way I find...
Poppy the purple unicorn

Her body is purple, her mane is violet, her horn is lilac
And best of all she's shiny
I walk over to her and we have an extremely long conversation
And in half an hour we are best friends

She introduced me to her queen
Who is as shiny as a diamond and as gold as a medal.

Eloise Jenkins (11)
St Teresa Catholic Primary School, Dagenham

A Random Dream

A m I running like the speeding Flash?

R andom stuff gives me an annoying rash
A nd dinosaurs are running in a dash
N aughty Cisco on my computer opening a tab
D ad gave him a sarcastic clap
O mega Savitar stabbed Kid Flash, my friend
M y friend is now dead, dead, dead

D oors open to what Flash read
R ight now I am seeing monsters eating my bed
E arbuds I give to myself
A nd now I see some elves
M y astronaut hears some ringing bells.

Karl Shane Vilar Antipuesto (11)
St Teresa Catholic Primary School, Dagenham

If I Could Be A...

If I could be a pirate, I would sail around on the deep, blue sea
If I were an astronaut, I would dance in space with glee

If I could be a writer, I would write the best stories
If I were a footballer, I would get a lot of glory

If I could be a wizard, I would make loads of bubbling potions
If I were a hairdresser, I would create numerous lotions

If I could be a teacher, I would teach forever
If I were a superhero, I would never say never.

Daisy Makumbi (10)
St Teresa Catholic Primary School, Dagenham

Dream Mr Unicorn

Dear Mr Unicorn,
I think I've found your horn,
It was chilling in the sky,
And hopefully you flew this high.

I was flying in the sky,
I spotted a rainbow high in the sky,
When I went there, it was a horn
I thought it was yours, Mr Unicorn.

Your glamorous blue eyes,
I could let the clouds rise,
Your multicoloured, swirly tail,
As swirly as a snail.

Your soft, glittery hair,
Which will make everyone stare,
As sparkly as a unicorn.

U nearthly creatures of ethereal beauty
N o one may see them, save those who are pure
I n legend and beauty they were created
C an one ever explain their powerful lure?
O ver and over their mysteries enchant me
R eal or imagined? Extinct or alive?
N ow and again I feel they protect me
S afeguarding my dreams, so that they may thrive.

Laiba Waqas (9)
Uphall Primary School, Ilford

Once Upon A Dream

O nce upon a dream
N othing was how it seemed
C autiously I strolled
E ver so quietly and bold

U nfortunately, I could not see anything to hold
P atiently I waited but then it became cold
O nce I realised it was very late
N o one would come, it was my fate

A spooky figure passed, it was frightening

D readfully, I followed it, suddenly there was lightning
R ealising the dangers ahead, I wished I was in bed
E xcruciatingly painful, but I got away
A wfully cold it seemed, although it was May
M iraculously, I woke up and in bed I lay.

Zobia Ramzan (11)
Uphall Primary School, Ilford

Monsters

M assive man-eating monster in my closet standing right in front of me
O ld and wrinkly, the monster is as big as it can be
N erve-tingling noise when it drags its claws along the door
S ilently, in a scary corner, I'm curled up right on the floor
T errified - I curl up into my bed
E very time I try to sleep, I see him in my head
R oaring thunder and lighting outside, I say, 'I've had enough.'
S o I open up the closet door and he vanishes into the cloud of puff.

Mohamed Diine (11)
Uphall Primary School, Ilford

Two Dreams Are Better Than One Nightmare

Come back little fairy
We haven't really met
I think your name is Mary
But I don't know you yet

There was a witch in my nightmare
Who was really, really mean
She would always stand and watch and stare
I felt like I was going to scream

Then a little fairy came
And made the bad things good
The ugly witch was very lame
Leaving her shredded flesh in blood

The little fairy went away
And now I know her name is May.

Faduma Ahmed (11)
Uphall Primary School, Ilford

Monster Teacher

I come to school every day
My teacher, Mrs Smith, is always there
We will never dare
Oh I swear
To laugh behind her back
Dropping a tissue on the bathroom floor
Watch out
Mrs Smith is about
Why are we so afraid? You may ask
Shh, Mrs Smith is a monster
She secretly sneaks sweets from the jars
I really want to send her to Mars!
But at the end of the day
There's always a way
To sneak out of class!

Aye Myant Naing (11)
Uphall Primary School, Ilford

Once Upon A Dream

D ream I did, every day, but this was the scariest, oh my days
R unning like a mouse, which is chased by a monster, who's a snake
E yes I tried to open, but nothing happened, that was the moment I fell down
'A aaa!' I said as he came in front of me
M y eyes opened and that was my dream.

Farhad Muhmmad Arshad (11)
Uphall Primary School, Ilford

Candyland

When I was little and I went to bed
A million thoughts swirled in my head
Some of them good, some of them bad
The scary ones that made me sad

My mummy would come in and lay with me
She'd talk about happier things to see
Bunnies and teddies and playing in the sand
We made up a world called Candy Land

Candyfloss clouds and a butterscotch sun
Gingerbread people having lots of fun
Hot chocolate rivers and lollipop trees
Chewing gum grass and gummy bear bees

Liquorice stems with bubblegum flowers
I could dream of all this for hours and hours
I still dream of this after all this time
I'm glad I could tell you all in this rhyme

So many sleeps left till I grow old
Mum tucking me in to keep out the cold
Candyland goes on for miles and miles
I'm happy that my mummy gave me these smiles.

James Wager (10)
White Court Primary School, Great Notley

Dreaming Of Dreaming

One thousand thoughts dance in my head
A million idea bubbles above my bed
But I try so hard to get to sleep
I'm even counting fluffy sheep

I wish that I could dream tonight
Of unicorns, aliens, a magnificent sight
Of butterflies, ponies, beautiful things
Or rivers of chocolate and golden rings

But the thoughts keep running around my head
Looking at the clock next to my bed
Still trying hard to get to sleep
Counting those little, fluffy sheep

I wish that I could dream again
Of a giant gummy bear or ten
Of magic cheese pizza that tastes so nice
While floating over snow and ice

But those thoughts still swimming in my head
Feel like there are rocks in my bed
Desperately trying to get to sleep
Now I'm fed up with those fluffy sheep

Suddenly, falling through marshmallow cloud
Cheered on by a roaring crowd
Hold on, I'm not in my bed
Finally, sleep and dreams have filled my head.

Mia Lily Sawyer (10)
White Court Primary School, Great Notley

Dream To Candyland

There is a girl named Sophie
Who dreams the strangest things
Last week she dreamt of an octopus
Who could juggle and then sing

This week she dreams of Candyland
And rabbits made of gel
And when she sniffs the air
There is a sugary smell

She opens her eyes with her cat named Pinky
Looking around for something stinky
Gummy bears and gummy bunnies
And unicorns with coloured tummies

But listen, there is a dragon crying
He's locked in a cage and its mystifying
There must be a way to get him out
Sophie will save him without a doubt

She calls her unicorn friend to help
Before the dragon begins to yelp
His name is Mr Rainbow Farts
And he likes eating strawberry tarts.

Sophie Louise Carpenter (10)
White Court Primary School, Great Notley

When I Flew

As I drifted out of maths, I was dropped into a sapphire sky
Stars, birds, clouds and hills I drifted by
I did tight corkscrews through loop-shaped clouds
And backflips with the birds
I shouted, 'This is great!' As I could not be heard
The moon cast its silver light across the tranquil sky
The moon in shape was circular and I asked myself why
Suddenly, a bird started saying my name repeatedly
I was confused at first but then I started rapidly falling
Everything seemed blurry until...
I woke up
I was in class doing maths
The teacher was saying my name
And I had fallen off my chair
From that day forwards I never fell asleep in class for I was in big trouble.

Samuel Paternoster (10)
White Court Primary School, Great Notley

Tingo And Me

I lift my head up high
When I'd had my luxurious lie
I was in the sky with Tingo
My only flying flamingo

How could I fly
In the painted black sky
Dotted with spectacular stars
Peering out to see the planet Mars

Tingo and me accidentally got pulled into the black hole
We stumbled across pirates and trolls
Past dinosaurs and aliens
I'm sure I saw a unicorn like my grandad Adrian

I'm back at home in my bed
Oh won't you wake up sleepy head?
Tingo's been snoring for a while
And when she'd woken up I'm sure I saw a smile.

Jasmine Rockenbach (10)
White Court Primary School, Great Notley

Nuclear

The finish line was in sight, all I felt was delight
All it gave was fright
But there wasn't anything I couldn't do
And that's really quite true.

Midway, trying to say, 'Hey,' to Mum,
'It's so much fun at the mud run
So I'm just staying here.'

Dad and Mum, having fun
All my friends reaching ends!
Blood, sweat and tears at the event
That's been on for years
Now it's just about time to say cheers
Celebrate
It's really great
Going to get a medal
Made out of metal
For a team with a huge dream!
Nuclear!

Harry Abbott (10)
White Court Primary School, Great Notley

Flying

I see planted in the air, fluffy clouds like coconut candyfloss
I see snowy white concord darting through the sky like a flash of lightning
I see a busy row of racing cars heading to the starting line like a moth to a light
I see placed on the cobbled path, Big Ben as high as ten giraffes
I see a tree in front of me... *whoosh! Bang!* Ouch!
I yawn and scrub my eyes and realise what had happened
I check for any wings and if I was hurt on anything
I look around to check the scene and look for that tree which was emerald green
It turned out when you see a bird, before you dream, it could be weirder than it seems!

Layla Huggins (10)
White Court Primary School, Great Notley

Once Upon A Dream

F eeling courageous and cautious
A nd believing in my dazzling dreams
M emorising my hard-practised rigid routines
O lympic stadium with spectacular crowds
U ntil that phenomenal final moment
S tanding high on the glamorous, glittering podium

G olden glinting medals like a prestigious spotlight
Y ellow, fluorescent sparkles planted on the walls
M ind-blowing magical powers
N ever-ending fame
A ll my dreams are coming true
S ilent, swishing air making me blush
T oday was the day my fame was real.

Ella Fay Brookes (9)
White Court Primary School, Great Notley

Imagine A World

I 'm flying through the air to a twinkling, neon land
M etallic stars paint the sky
A s kaleidoscopic mermaids rest on the sand
G enius giants stomping through colossal, verdant valleys
I swim through clouds and ask myself, 'Is this whole world doo-lally?'
N othing is more fascinating than this picturesque world I'm in
A t last I'm here, at last I see
T all sapphire towers welcome me
I see fluorescent fairies, red and blue
O ctopuses raise their tentacles in salute
N o, no, this can't be true!

Elodie Dobson (9)
White Court Primary School, Great Notley

The Swan Lake

The marvellous moon shone brightly
It bounced into the lake like a nice light and a mirror
In sight of the swaying, glistening lake, there was the prettiest swan I had ever seen
Although the swan was beautiful, she had an extremely sad face
I even think she was crying!

Suddenly, I saw her amazingly transform into a beautiful girl with long, golden hair
She gracefully started dancing
When the sun came back up she changed back into a swan
In a blink of an eye, a prince came with two fairies
And the fairies had a wand and transformed her back into a girl once more.

Abigail Milner (9)
White Court Primary School, Great Notley

Dream World

D iamond unicorns I see sparkling in the sunshine
R iding a pink unicorn while eating candy
E ating my sweets in Unicorn Candy Land
A golden bunny hops around the bubblegum flowers
M y imaginary friend is there

W aiting for me to pick some bubblegum flowers
O n the way to the flowers I spotted a silver and gold unicorn
R ight out of the corner of my eye I see my imaginary friend is fascinated
L aughing at this special unicorn doing a boogie
D o you think you would like to come to my dream world?

Emily Raven (10)
White Court Primary School, Great Notley

Clown Woods

C reepily I strolled into the woods
L osing my patience I was scared, especially in my childhood
'O h my God,' I screamed. There was a clown
W alking closer, he stalked us. I had a frown
N ow the clown's glowing luminous eyes turned red

W hen will it stop? It was in my head
O xygen is lost, it's not a game
O fficially it was not the same
'D ead we are,' I quietly said
S uddenly, I woke up in my cosy bed.

Jack James Adams (10)
White Court Primary School, Great Notley

A Fishy Adventure

F irst I see a water palace, yet somehow I haven't drowned
R ight then is when something evil growled
I n fear I run, but there's nowhere to hide
G uess what? Out of nowhere, there appeared a guide
H e said, 'Face the dragon, use your might.'
T hen I got the feeling of fright
E very limb was frozen in shock
N ext a dragon appeared, as wide as a loch
E ventually it dived, leaving me screaming
D on't worry though, it turned out I was dreaming!

David Horobin (10)
White Court Primary School, Great Notley

Football Dream

As I walked into this mysterious stadium
All I could see were eyes glaring at me
A stern-looking referee to toughen up the game
Tensed to see, I was in the FA Cup Final
Standing on the pitch
Suddenly, the game starts and in two minutes I score three goals
To make it 3-0 to us
My teammates around, pressuring me
Then the other team make it 3-3
Then I am awarded a penalty in the 90th minute
The most nerve wracking thing in my life
I step up to take it
Bam, in no time I score the winning goal...

Cameron Dawes (10)
White Court Primary School, Great Notley

Should I Do It?

I close my eyes and get in bed
I feel weird with a shiver down my spine
I get out of bed, my house is very different
I come out of my house
More than 30 people outside my house saying, 'Will you join?'
I am freaked, I find out I got scouted for Clown FC
I had no clue what that was
Were they messing around but no
That night clowns came to my house
I punched myself!
Next morning clowns at the stadium
They say, 'Get up, get up!'
I fell over and woke up in my house
What happened?

Eli Green (10)
White Court Primary School, Great Notley

Faraway

I was far away on an ice peak
Looking around, I felt ever so weak
As this land was ever so huge
And I spotted an unholy ooze

But what's this I see?
Wait!
It's coming straight for me!
It was a roller coaster on a war path
My heart was starting to race
But just as I was about to brace
It stopped the chase
I quickly move out of the way

The scenery around me is beautiful
As beautiful as it gets
And then I wonder
Why haven't I woken up yet?

Callum Orton (10)
White Court Primary School, Great Notley

Drive Sports Car

D anger for some, excitement for others
R ecreating history in the making
I n the driver's seat I sat
V icious engine noise
E xcitement in the air

S uper steering
P ulls like a Ferrari
O ff to Sport +
R uns like the wind
T urn up the volume
S pectacular tunes on the radio

C razy drifts on the gravel track
A ccurate distances
R epeat every day for super dreams.

Henry Payne (10)
White Court Primary School, Great Notley

I Am A Footballer

I could see the crowd screaming
I could see the ball moving
I could see the grass swaying
I could see the players running

I am at the place of my dreams
I am at my dream house
I am at a football stadium

I get what I like
I get what is fabulous
I get a hat-trick

I am with my dream friends
I am with quality
I am with Manchester United

I don't feel sad
I don't feel good
I feel great.

Tom Parker (10)
White Court Primary School, Great Notley

The Epic Dragon

T he dragon is my companion
H e is my best friend
E verything we do together

E ndless journeys we make
P arts are sad, parts are good
I 'm my dragon and he is me
C ars are not real in the world yet

D eadly is he
R aging fire breath
A monster to others
G entle to me, is my best friend
O ur bond will last forever
N ever to part.

Harry George Russell (10)
White Court Primary School, Great Notley

Ulsa And The Unicorn Crew

Hello Ulsa Unicorn
I came to you today
How the clouds are cotton candy
I want to go to meet your friend Randy

Your group of wonderful sights
Oh I just can't wait to see them
The bright colours and personality
That just makes you who you are
You're that loving superstar

Let me go visit that rainbow
The one that was smiling at me
I had to try some of that candy
I could just see it looking at me.

Kathryn Edwards (10)
White Court Primary School, Great Notley

My Dream

Once upon a dream
With my friends and Donald Trump
Glancing at the old London with my eyes
Seeing Mo Farah and Mike Tyson

Once upon a dream
In London, feeling...
Feeling humorous and enjoyable
Feeling funny and hyped

Once upon a dream
In a terrorist attack
Hear gunfire and screaming
Smelling smoke and fire

Once upon a dream
As dreams are weird
But all dreams are crazy.

Joe Wiltshire (10)
White Court Primary School, Great Notley

The Hero Saves The Nightmare

I'm the dashing princess
Locked up in the castle
The flaring beast won't let me free
My knight in shining armour
Then cautiously winks down at me

After one mighty slash
I am released from my prison
As we danced together through the sunset
The silver moon had risen

Not all fairy tales end well
Some could be a true disaster
But now I am pleased to say
This one ended with a happy every after!

Verity Lucas (9)
White Court Primary School, Great Notley

Magnificent Moon Full Of Dreamcatching

The moon had formed
The stars are now out of their hideaway
Let's dance the night away

Across the purple tippled water
I saw the silver spotted moon
Gently blow a kiss to all the sleeping children

Half of you as dark as a panda
Black spots
You gently smother moonlight over my delicate dream bottles

Dreams, stop now you have been captured
Come into the jar, come, come.

Aishwari Patel (9)
White Court Primary School, Great Notley

Travelling Through Space

I could spot aliens dancing on Mars
Whilst stars twinkle in the sky
I spotted all of the planets in the solar system
I've always dreamed of coming here, but why?

I flew there by rocket
And took pictures of the stars
There was lots to see in space
including the craters on Mars

Where have I landed?
I have landed on the moon
It might be far, far away
I may return there soon.

Joshua Young (10)
White Court Primary School, Great Notley

Silver Streams

S uper sights
I n the far distance
L icking the Earth
V icious if you're below
E merging from the horizon
R eaching the Earth's limit

S pectacular streams
T ouching my fingertips
R unning from the fire
E scaping its grip
A mazing streams finding the surface
M arvellous, it really is
S o marvellous.

Dillon Gold (10)
White Court Primary School, Great Notley

Football!

I can't believe I'm here at White Hart Lane ground
The stadium is amazing and everyone's so loud
The epic pitch is made of Skittles
The goal looks so little

I'm so excited playing with Harry Kane
But sometimes he can be a pain
I've got to take a penalty
Oh no, it's all down to me

The ball is screaming
I must be dreaming
The ball goes in
Our team wins.

Rhiannon Gray (10)
White Court Primary School, Great Notley

If I Could Fly!

If I could fly up high with the birds
I would go to places of which I have heard
New York City is where I would head
As I lay there in my bed
If I could fly up in the sky
I would watch as the clouds float by
I would look out for bad guys roaming the street
I would defeat them with my stinky feet
If I could fly, how happy I would be
With the wind whizzing around me
I must not do a wee!

Charlie Haynes (10)
White Court Primary School, Great Notley

The Dream

I have a dream
Of going to space
I picture it in my mind as I dream

I picture in my mind my fellow astronauts
I picture the stars and Earth from above
I feel nervous but excited

I picture Jupiter and Uranus
Then I witness a solar eclipse
It was astounding and beautiful

I picture the galaxy
I wake up shocked
I had a dream.

Luke Croker (10)
White Court Primary School, Great Notley

Unicorns Vs Dinosaurs

I was in the dinosaur times, watching dinosaurs dancing
I was with a unicorn named Lunacorn
We were in the dinosaurs' country in the dinosaur times
I felt excited, a little bit scared, terrified and astonished
Lunacorn uses magical unicorn powers and sends the dinosaurs chasing me
The dinosaurs eventually slow down and we are safe at last.

Saffron Lily Rose Hockley-Warner (10)
White Court Primary School, Great Notley

Night

Night
No light
I can't fly my kite
Bed clothes hold me tight
In my room out of sight
Make sure the bed bugs don't bite
Keep my eyes closed with all my might
With my imagination I do fight
Trying not to glance left or right
Hoping not to get a fright
In my bed, in my room at night.

Adam Brathwaite (9)
White Court Primary School, Great Notley

The Never-Ending Game

F ear of failing to succeed
O f trying always to believe
O pposition everywhere
T rying not to care
B lood, sweat and tears
A re given all through the years
L ooking always at the team
L iving the never-ending dream.

Ryan Young (10)
White Court Primary School, Great Notley

My Dream Friend!

There once was a horse who had a horn
He was my very own unicorn!
We played in my dreams
All night it seemed
Until the morning
Then he left without warning
And when I went to sleep again
He was my magical, mystical dream friend.

Mia Ozcan (10)
White Court Primary School, Great Notley

YoungWriters
Est.1991

YOUNG WRITERS INFORMATION

We hope you have enjoyed reading this book – and that you will continue to in the coming years.

If you're a young writer who enjoys reading and creative writing, or the parent of an enthusiastic poet or story writer, do visit our website **www.youngwriters.co.uk**. Here you will find free competitions, workshops and games, as well as recommended reads, a poetry glossary and our blog.

If you would like to order further copies of this book, or any of our other titles, then please give us a call or visit **www.youngwriters.co.uk**.

Young Writers
Remus House
Coltsfoot Drive
Peterborough
PE2 9BF
(01733) 890066
info@youngwriters.co.uk